620 Days

By

Charles F. Callihan

TABLE OF CONTENTS

Forward

This book was written from a journal I started the first evening I entered the prison, known as Beaumont Low. The journal is in the form of daily letters I wrote to my wife. She kept them in chronological order, and upon my return home, to home confinement, I wrote this book based on entries in the journal.

Events depicted in this book are grouped into categories rather than in the order in which they occurred. Prison life is not one big event or crisis after another. Instead, it is days of monotony and routine followed by a big event or crisis that I, or anyone else present, could not have predicted the event, the exact time, the cause or the magnitude of the response to the event. In prison, there is always a foreboding pall that hangs over every activity, no matter how mondain. This is because you always know the calm you are experiencing is always the calm before the storm.

In prison there is always the feeling present between the members of your group, whether cartel or gang, that "we are in it together" and "I'm going to watch out for you because I know you are watching out for me." When you see your fellow group member or members during the day, there is always a smile and a feeling of "family." The short period of time I was in the custody of the BOP, I nevertheless, formed an attachment to the men in my group, the White Guys in barracks UB in Beaumont Low. When I left, it felt (and still feels) like I left my friends in a predicament, like I left them in car wreck.

I know that Harold, Sam, Wilbur, Lawrence, and a few others are doing what they were doing before I came and will continue their respective routines for several more years, and in some instances, several more decades before it is their turn to leave or die. I think of them every day, but that habit will, I am sure, become weaker over time and eventually a significant period of time will pass before I inadvertently think of them. It is the same process that occurs when you are separated from a loved one permanently, or for an extended period of time.

Prologue

I had a career as a chemical engineer with an MBA that spanned forty-five years. Along the way I moved every few years as I was transferred within my company or moved to a better position with another company. Over the course of my career, moves took me from Missouri to Michigan, Georgia, Missouri (again), Arkansas, Pennsylvania, Kentucky, Ohio, New Jersey, Louisiana and finally Texas.

It was in Louisiana on March 10, 2010 that I took the "odd" job. A position that was apart from the chemical and petro-chemical positions typical for a chemical engineer. It was a demil company, short for demilitarization company, named Explo Systems, Inc. in Minden, Louisiana. A demil company takes munitions and ordnance[1] from the Department of Defense and renders them unusable for their original purpose by disposing of them by detonation or by re-engineering them for commercial use. For example, altering a military explosive so it can be sold to a mining company as a commercial explosive.

I took the job because the pay was far more than competing companies' offerings for a Vice-President of environmental affairs – one in North Carolina and one in Mississippi. I took the Explo Systems position as Director of Technology. The cost of living in Shreveport, Louisiana compared to Clayton, New Jersey where we were living, coupled with the salary, made it very monetarily attractive. Beyond the monetary lure, was the chance to do something different, something patriotic (defense related), and something that just makes you feel good, e.g., taking something designed for death and

---

[1] munitions – materials used in war, especially weapons and ammunition

ordnance – means of delivery for munitions...such as propellant charges for artillery shells destruction and rendering it harmless or refocusing it toward beneficial re-use.

I was completely oblivious to the fact that Explo Systems, Inc. was a criminal organization that had been operating in this fashion beginning about 2004. I left Explo Systems on May 17, 2013 never knowing of their criminal enterprise. Munitions and ordnance were brought in and dismantled with systems I designed. They would dismantle part of what was sent, falsify records of the quantity dismantled, and literally hide what was not demilled in the vast expanse of forest and munitions bunkers that make up Camp Minden. Truckloads of artillery propellant charges and other military munitions and ordnance were hidden in this manner. One is not supposed to drive aimlessly about in a military installation, so I never explored the remote areas because I was not authorized to do so and had no reason to do so. I remained blissfully unaware of the criminal conspiracy and activities occurring daily around me.

Although I was not a part of the criminal conspiracy (the Feds acknowledge this too), because I worked closely with those who were a part of the conspiracy, I should have known what was going on, according to the Federal prosecutor. My attorney, during my legal struggle to stay out of jail, said it best,

"It is equivalent to, if you worked in a bank and the senior managers of the bank were stealing from the bank. Since you worked with them daily you should have known about it."

My attorney was confident that I would be found innocent if it went to trial up until the Friday before the trial that was to begin on the following Monday. The turning point on that Friday in June 2018 was the suicide of the President of Explo

Systems in the early afternoon. And, sometime over the weekend, the Vice-President of Operations attempted suicide. Of the top six managers and owners of Explo Systems who were going to trial, the top two had either committed suicide or attempted it. Of the remaining four defendants, the next in line in the hierarchy was me. The trial was postponed for a week and my attorney met with the prosecution and then said to me,

"After the suicide and attempted suicide, it is certain a jury will convict the remaining defendants and the prosecution has offered you a plea deal. The prosecution will drop the conspiracy charge, but you must plead guilty to something else. It will carry a twenty-four-month sentence instead of a minimum sixty-month sentence. I recommend you take this plea agreement."

I took the plea agreement and served 441 days at a Federal Low Security Prison – Bloody Beaumont – along with 108 days at a halfway house – Leidel – and 71 days in home confinement — 620 days total. My home confinement ended on September 25, 2020 and I have twelve months of probation which ends about August 25, 2021.

This book is an account of my experience – a little over twenty months in the Federal Bureau of Prisons custody. All of the events described are true in the sense that I witnessed them, or they were told to me as truth. Some events I heard from other inmates as stories and have no way of saying they are true. However, from the stories in here that I witnessed, it seems to me that the stranger the stories the more likely it is that they are true. The reason is that no one, including me, can have the imagination to come up with what I witnessed, heard about as truth, and experienced. Ask anyone who has been "in the joint" for any length of time about anything I have written in this book and they will tell you, "It smacks of truth." All names have been changed except the names of the companies I mention, and my name. The prison and halfway house descriptions are true and accurate. In some instances, I have combined two characters into one because it makes the story easier to tell and understand.

There is no hidden agenda. It is simply my best effort at describing what happened to me, my family and by extension, my closest friends that helped us survive what some might call an ordeal. It also provides an honest portrayal of what prison life is like in a low security federal prison and halfway house. I do not count it as an ordeal when compared to terminal illness, war, famine or the death or disabling of loved ones. Early on in my prison life I tried as best I could to become a "casual observer of human behavior" because I remembered reading about it in a book as a teenager, and I can no longer remember the title of the book.

The book I had read was a true story about life in a Nazi prisoner of war camp as told by an American airman shot down over Germany in 1943. Every day the Nazi guards would march all the prisoners around the perimeter of the stockade in all kinds of weather with minimal clothing against the cold, snow, sleet and rain. During the march, there was a long stretch of the path that came within ten feet of the high voltage wired perimeter fence. If a prisoner wanted to end it all, he simply had to step out of line, walk ten feet and touch the wire. Three or four times per week, someone did just that. In fact, the guards would wager how many would do it during the week. The hero and teller of the story, to survive, adopted the casual observer of human behavior attitude so that he did not become too emotionally involved with what he witnessed and experienced daily. I recall he said that he consciously pretended he was an actor in a movie, and he was just playing a character, following a script. He survived a year and a half in horrible conditions. I tried to adopt this same attitude because I knew it would not be as bad as a World War II Nazi prison camp, so if it worked for him, it would work for me, and it did.

The stories of the men I encountered while in prison cover the extremes of human behavior, from incredibly good, to definitive evil, to simply deranged.

Chapter I
Transition from Alcan Pharma Packaging to Explo Systems Inc.

This is my story...

In June 2006, I accepted a position as Manager of Health, Safety and Environmental Affairs for North America with Alcan Pharma Packaging in Vineland, New Jersey. The position required travel throughout the United States and Canada on a regular basis. Almost monthly, I would travel to Chase City, Virginia, and the next week to Syracuse, Nebraska, then Indianapolis, Indiana, then Montreal, Quebec and finally Ajax, Ontario (suburb of Toronto). The order would vary month to month, but the weekly trips were constant. There were two plants in New Jersey, and I would spend a week visiting them and then two or three days weekly "on the road." Alcan made packaging for pharmaceuticals as the name suggests. Thousands of glass insulin vials were manufactured daily at each plant. Some plants made plastic syringes while other plants made sterile bags for plasma. The company was a major supplier to the "Medical Injectable" industry. That is, anything that a person, medical professional or individual, sticks a needle into in order to draw in a dose of a pharmaceutical that is then injected into the human or animal body.

My job as Manager of Health, Safety and Environmental Affairs for North America was to ensure adequate training for employees, review accidents/injuries and inspect the facility for compliance with Food and Drug Administration pharmaceutical packaging hygiene and housekeeping requirements at manufacturing sites in the United States and Canada. I liked the job, including the travel, and it was the heart of my career in that I had similar jobs with previous companies, though not as many sites to visit and none routinely out of the country.

Alcan Pharma Packaging was headquartered in Montreal, Quebec but they also had manufacturing facilities in Europe (France and Germany), and I got to travel to Paris about three times per year for a world-wide EHS (Environmental, Health and Safety) conference. Life was good, but it all came to a halt when Rio Tinto, an Australian company, purchased Alcan Pharma Packaging in October 2009. As usually happens to senior management in a company that is purchased, I was given a severance package and shown the door. I was used to this and I knew within three months I would find another job and the generous severance package meant I would be better off financially then if my job with Alcan had just continued unchanged.

I contacted three headhunter firms (placement firms for executives) with my updated resume and what type of job I was looking for. I had always preferred environmental affairs over safety and health, but usually the two were combined in one position so I would get the top division or corporate EHS position. I always said I did not change jobs, I changed companies; it is the same job. As usual, I got eight "hits" within the first two weeks of my job search. It is then my happy task to sift through the offers of interviews and pick two or three and then begin the interview process. I actually enjoyed this part; it is like being courted by several attractive entities at the same time. My wife liked it too, because the agreement we have is that if she is willing to follow me around the country, she can pick the house and neighborhood within a price ceiling and she enjoyed searching the internet in the city where the job is located and lining up realtors for me to contact when I came to town to interview. In some instances, the company would pay for her to travel with me on the interview to ensure she would like the location where we would live.

My wife and I had learned the hard way to not be too quick to pick a house, buy it and move in. In one instance, after about three months of exploring our new city, we stumbled on an area of the city much more attractive than where we had moved, and we would have purchased a home there had we known about it. Therefore, we usually rented an apartment – a three-month lease – if we could, and then happily we explored our new surroundings.

I sifted through eight offers of interviews and picked three – one in North Carolina, one in Mississippi and one in Louisiana. All of them were either environmental related or engineering with some environmental. I would have for the first time in a longtime the luxury of not having to deal with safety and health managerial issues as a part of my job. I was excited about the prospects. The "odd" job was the one near Minden, Louisiana a small city near Shreveport where it was recommended that we live. Minden's claim to fame is that it is the town where the outlaws Bonnie and Clyde met their fate. For years there was a Bonnie and Clyde museum just off the town square where you could see photographs of the outlaws and the centerpiece of the museum was their bullet ridden car where their lives had ended just outside Minden.

Also, just outside Minden, was an army camp operated by the Louisiana National Guard. The camp had once been known as the Louisiana Army Ammunition Depot where they manufactured 155mm artillery shells. The camp was operated in this manner during World War II, the Korean War, and the Viet Nam War. They also at one time had manufactured TNT and Tritonal.[2]

Camp Minden is now utilized by the Army Reserve to train a transportation company (train personnel to drive trucks), military police, and an air support operations squadron. And, in other areas they leased buildings, grounds and bunkers to private firms to dismantle military munitions and ordnance or to manufacture black powder (gun powder). One of the private firms that dismantled military munitions and ordnance – demil – was Explo Systems, Inc. Explo Systems needed a chemical engineer to design systems to safely dismantle artillery shells, bombs, and mines and also obtain appropriate permits for these operations with the LDEQ (Louisiana Department of Environmental Quality) and the US-EPA (United States Environmental Protection Agency). Unfortunately, of the three companies courting me, I picked Explo Systems. In fact, they appeared so attractive, from a monetary, novelty and location perspective, I abandoned the interview process with the other two firms that were interested in me. BIG MISTAKE...however, I did not know this until years later.

I interviewed Explo and really liked everyone who interviewed me. They seemed incredibly happy that I was interested in the job they had in mind for me. It was funny that the President of Explo (also one of the owners), the Vice-President (the other

---

[2] TNT – 2,4,6-Trinitrotoluene or $C_6H_2(NO_2)_3CH_3$ – is a yellow solid explosive that in flake form resembles frosted corn flakes but with a rubbery feel and pungent aroma like strong yeast. Tritonal – a military explosive — a mixture of 80% TNT and 20% Aluminum powder. Tritonal is 18% more destructive than an equivalent amount of TNT and the Aluminum powder causes fires that are difficult, if not impossible, to be extinguished with water. Tritonal is used to destroy ships and create firestorms in cities.

owner) and the Manufacturing Manager all were named Larry – you cannot make this stuff up. I flew back to New Jersey, told my wife how attractive the job and offer were and how much money she could spend on a house. She took an evening and searched the internet in Shreveport and found beautiful houses that in New Jersey would have been far beyond what we could afford, but in Shreveport, they were not even near the top of what we could afford. We jumped aboard the Explo bandwagon with high hopes and expectations.

Chapter II
The World of Demil

The world of demil was unlike anything I had ever experienced before. The concept of taking an artillery shell, bomb or mine and taking it apart safely and selling the components was nothing like managing a chemical process in a chemical or refining manufacturing site. However, chemical engineering principles remain the same, that is, understand the process and the chemical reactions that you want to occur, or in this case, the chemical reactions you do not want to occur. Then, put in place safeguards to prevent the occurrence of what you do not want to happen, and also put in place a process that causes what you do want to happen. And do it over and over again until you run out of artillery shells or bombs or mines or whatever it is that is being demilled. It sounds simple and in reality, if done correctly, it is simple.

For example, I would compare it to a ballet if you went to a performance of the Nut Cracker on a Sunday afternoon and twenty minutes into the performance you snapped a picture it would have a certain number of people on stage and they would be jumping or standing or otherwise moving around. Then, if you went back for the evening performance and snapped a picture twenty minutes into the performance and compared the evening performance picture with the afternoon's picture it is likely the pictures would be substantially identical. Even if they were not entirely the same performers, if they were playing a particular part, they would be performing the same in each performance. The key to dismantling munitions and ordnance in a safe manner is identical in practice to managing a hazardous chemical reaction day after day in a chemical or petro-chemical manufacturing environment. That is, figure out how to do it safely and put in safe guards, alarms, protocols, and procedures that ensure, as much as is humanly possible, to always perform the operation or manage the process in the same manner day after day, no matter who is performing the various tasks that make up the total process.

After I got over the fact that live munitions in the form of bombs were the raw material of the process, the day to day operation was identical to operating a hazardous chemical reaction continuously day after day. The first time I walked into a bomb storage bunker and saw what was inside, I felt the hair on the back of my neck stand up and I thought, “What have I gotten myself into.”

Entrance to one of the Dozens of Bunkers at Camp Minden

Typical Contents of a Bunker at Camp Minden

Then, after I talked to my co-workers, those within the conspiracy, I realized it truly was no different than a refinery or other chemical manufacturing process. A bomb when it explodes is housing a chemical reaction for a few milliseconds. The task in a refinery, which can be a bomb, is to harness the reaction safely and continuously. In a demil process, the task is to prevent the bomb's potential chemical reaction from occurring at all. Just harness the reaction and keep it from occurring.

Bombs, such as the 500- and 750-pound bombs shown below are dismantled in either one of two ways: Machine, Crack and Melt or Cryofracture with Water Separation. The Machine, Crack and Melt process was in place upon my arrival and it was slow, but demonstrably safe, in that thousands of bombs had been demilled via this process prior to my arrival and none of them had exploded during the process.

Bomb Being Placed in Lathe

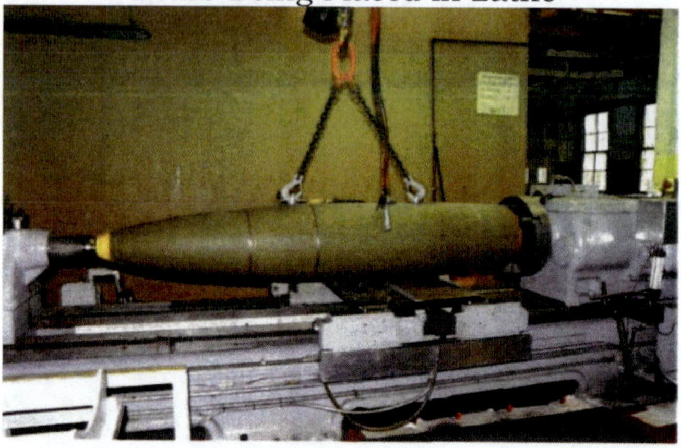

Bomb After Being Scoured Four Places by Lathe

Bomb Being Cracked Along the Scour Cuts by Press

Bomb After Cracking

Center Section of Bomb Being Pressed Out

Bomb Nose Section in Steam Bath

Regardless of the method utilized to dismantle the bombs, the resultant contents were melted at 177°F. The melted or molten TNT is poured over a chilled (40°F) rotating cylinder in a thin film, on a piece of equipment called a Flaker.

Flaker

The TNT melts in a sheet that is continuously broken at the end of the cylinder into the flakes, shown below. Flaked TNT is placed in a polyethylene lined box in either 20 kilograms (44 pounds) or 40 pounds, depending on the customer's preference. TNT, packaged in this manner, is a commercial explosive utilized for mining and tunnel construction.

Finished TNT Product After Flaker (commercial explosive)

In the case of Tritonal (80%TNT and 20% Aluminum powder, a military explosive), there is a separation step where the molten TNT is separated from the Aluminum powder. The TNT is then processed in the flaker and the Aluminum powder is collected and sold to makers of reflective paint such as used on highway curbs and centerlines. The steel from the bomb is sold to a foundry licensed to accept steel that may have trace amounts of explosive on it. The final ordnance demil process in place at Explo was the dismantling of 155mm artillery propellant charges. A 155mm howitzer is a cannon with a crew of seven men...

155mm Howitzer

The propellant charge is contained within a rayon and cotton bag...

Propellant Charge Bag

The bag was lined with an elemental lead sheet and contained M6 Propellant pictured below.

M6 Propellant

M6 Propellant looks and feels like rabbit food, but if a spark or significant impact, like hitting a pellet with a hammer occurs, the propellant explodes like this...

Detonation of M6 Propellant

A full charge sends the 95-pound 155mm diameter artillery shell downrange as far as 15 miles. It detonates with a casualty radius of 109 yards with a kill zone radius of 55 yards. Other items in the propellant charge bag are black powder which at night does a good job of hiding muzzle flash and Ammonium Sulfate, $(NH_4)_2SO_4$.

Ammonium Sulfate acts as a lubricant so the barrel does not heat up as quickly as it would without the lubricant. Ammonium Sulfate allows more rounds to be sent down range before firing must cease to allow the barrel to cool. Ammonium Sulfate is and was, sold as a fertilizer for soybeans.

This was the work-a-day world I walked into and I enjoyed the job. I knew what was being sent to the dismantling or demil line daily for bombs and propellant charges. I knew what was being bid on for mortar and artillery rounds and I was assured these munitions would be forthcoming. What I did not know was that about 15 percent (my estimate after the fact) of what the Defense Department sent was being stored in the woods and magazines at Camp Minden, but the Defense Department was being billed for all that was being sent as if it had all been demilled.

Chapter III
The Day the Music Died

I awoke as usual on Tuesday, October 16, 2012 ate breakfast and headed for work about 6:45 AM. The news on the car radio "rocked my world." No one from Explo had notified me of anything amiss. The news stated some version of the following...

That on Monday at 11:40 PM, October 15, 2012, one of 98 storage bunkers at the Explo Systems Inc. site exploded prompting investigations by the EPA, LDEQ, the Louisiana State Police, and other responders. The explosion shattered windows in the City of Minden, Louisiana (approximately four miles to the northeast), and generated a 7,000-foot high mushroom cloud. Explo Systems was under contract with the Department of Army to demilitarize surplus munitions.[3]

When I got to work, I was told by my boss, the Vice-President of Operations, to go home and await further instructions and that my salary would continue. In subsequent weeks, I learned the following from watching news casts and reading the local paper.

The State Police found 10 million pounds of unsecured M6 (howitzer propellant) improperly stored outside of the bunkers and 8 million pounds of a variety of other explosives improperly stored inside bunkers. To keep the residents safe due to the potential risk, the town of Doyline, Louisiana (approximately 400 homes), was evacuated during operational hours from November 28

---

[3]https://www.epa.gov/sites/production/files/2015-03/documents/9544798

to December 7, 2013. In addition, the Youth Challenge Program (school) and non-essential personnel at Camp Minden were evacuated. The Webster Parish Jail at Camp Minden followed shelter-in-place procedures. The State Police directed Explo Systems, Inc., to temporarily secure the M6 in available bunkers.

In early November 2012, I began to search for employment since it was apparent to me that a lot of what was occurring at Explo Systems were things I had no idea about. I took my time since I was still receiving my salary and in early May I accepted a position with a large chemical manufacturer in Houston, Texas (270 miles southeast of Shreveport, Louisiana) as Vice-President of Environmental, Health, and Safety. We were moving to Houston, Texas and putting Explo Systems, Inc. behind us, or so I thought. Explo Systems declared bankruptcy in May 2013 and in August 2013, the Louisiana Military Department took ownership of the explosives at Explo Systems. The US-EPA initiated negotiations with all potentially responsible parties to eliminate the risks posed by the eighteen million pounds of M6 and other explosives.

My wife and I settled into our house in a suburb of southeast Houston and I began my job with a conventional chemical manufacturer without regard for what was occurring to the remnants of Explo Systems and Camp Minden. After about a year into my position, I decided to teach part-time three evenings a week at a local trade school, Remington College, in the Process Technology Department. I started teaching three nights per week and enjoyed it immensely.

In late August 2015, I do not remember the exact date, but the indictment is dated August 15, 2015, a US Marshall and a representative from the US-EPA came to my office and served me with a Federal Indictment. It is 27 pages long and had my name everywhere the other defendant's names were as part of a criminal conspiracy. The details were laid out in the indictment and all of it was news to me. Clearly to me, I was not a part of the conspiracy, but just as clearly, the US-EPA thought I was. Eventually, since there was no evidence of me being in the conspiracy, e.g., no documents, those in the conspiracy to their credit, also said I was not a part of the conspiracy, the Feds dropped the conspiracy charge against me. I had hired on after all of the others were hired by several years and documents produced showing they were all part of the conspiracy were dated prior to my beginning employment with Explo Systems. I was, however, still on the hook as someone "who should have known what was going on."

On page 16 of the indictment, these words eventually got me sentenced to twenty-four months in the Federal Prison System.

"LARRY SMITH, LARRY ANDREWS, ROBERT SIMON, DAVID ARVIDSON, and CHARLES FERRIS CALLIHAN caused the illegal transportation and disposal of D003 reactive hazardous waste generated from the processing of Type II explosive materials to unpermitted non-hazardous waste landfills in Louisiana and Arkansas to make room for M6 propellant..."

Arkansas landfill shipments of this material occurred prior to my employment. Shipments to the Louisiana landfill occurred while I was employed. I emphasized to my colleagues that material shipped to the Louisiana landfill must be non-reactive. That is, have so little explosive residue contained in the cardboard and plastic debris from shipping containers and demil operations that it would be indistinguishable from material that had never been in contact with explosives. I even spot checked the first shipments and they were fine. My trust level was much higher than it should have been, but I had never had any trust issues in waste shipments in my career and they all seemed eager to please. However, after my initial inspections, they shipped everything they wanted to ship regardless of the amount of explosive residue it contained. Yes, in hindsight, I should have been far less trusting and far more attentive to the point of blowing the whistle long, loud and clear. At the time, I was blissfully unaware of what I should have been doing. Ultimately, sentences handed down on November 28, 2018 to the managers and owners of Explo Systems, Inc. were:

President/Owner – Larry Andrews – no sentence due to suicide
Vice-President Operations – Robert Simon – 60 months – Fined $149,033
Vice-President/Owner – Larry Jackson – 55 months – Fined $34,800,000
Program Manager – David Arvidson – 45 months – Fined $149,032
Transportation Manager – Arthur Simpson – 41 months – Fined $92,921
Director Technology – Charles Callihan – 24 months – Fined $207,600

We were told that we would be informed of where to report by registered letter and the report date would be January 14, 2019 by 2:00 PM. My family and I prepared for my departure.

In January 2019, the Federal Government shutdown due to budget disagreements between the Congress and Executive Branches. On January 10th, four days from my report date I had not been informed of where to report. I called the US Marshall's office in Shreveport and said,

"Where do I report on January 14th, no one has told me."

The lady at the other end of the phone actually apologized and said someone would call me back. About four hours later another lady called and said report to Beaumont Low by 2:00 PM on January 14, 2019. She also said that since there was not enough time for a registered letter, she would send me an email with these instructions and I should acknowledge it, which I did.

My son drove from Jacksonville, Florida where he lives to Houston, Texas during the first week of January. You drive through Beaumont, Texas to get to Houston from Jacksonville. On January 14th, on his way back to Jacksonville, he dropped me off at the Federal Prison in Beaumont – commonly referred to by inmates and guards as "Bloody Beaumont." I got out of the car at 12:30 PM on January 14, 2019 walked through the front door and handed the guard behind the reception desk the letter the US Marshalls service had attached to their email directing me to report to Beaumont Low[4]. My twenty-four-month prison sentence had begun.

---

[4] The Federal Prison at Beaumont, Texas is an all-male inmate facility consisting of a maximum, medium and low security prisons plus a camp. For the maximum, medium and low security prisons, there is a punishment unit for each. The punishment unit is referred to as the "SHU" (pronounced "shoe") for Special Housing Unit. The SHU unit is described later in detail.

Chapter IV

Prison Life

Entrance to Beaumont Low
(Federal Prison in Beaumont, Texas)

When you are told to report to prison, you are also told what you can bring, and only what you can bring. I was told by the US Marshall lady in the same phone call that told me to report to Beaumont Low to only bring my prescription medication for my heart condition, my CPAP (Continuous Positive Airway Pressure) unit as I also have Sleep Apnea, and the clothes on my back. I walked into the front door, handed the guard at the front desk the letter I had been sent in the email from the US Marshall's service. The guard read the letter, handed it to another guard and she told me to go behind the screen at the end of the room and take off my clothes and put them in the clear trash bag she handed me. Behind the screen I would find the temporary clothes and slip on tennis shoes I was to wear until I could go to "Clothing" where I would be given my permanent uniforms and boots. I was also photographed and given a temporary ID Card that I was to keep on my person at all times.

After fifteen minutes, I had on my temporary uniform, my prescription medications in a small plastic bag and my CPAP unit in a small box they provided. I was escorted through the receiving department to "The Yard."

Beaumont Low

Beaumont Low, in all of its glory is shown above.[5] The yard is a twenty-acre field with several intertwining sidewalks on it. Sidewalks with a yellow stripe in the center are where inmates can walk. Sidewalks with a red line at the beginning are where inmates cannot walk. I was beginning to feel "special." The guard pointed at the center of three buildings, called barracks. All barracks buildings are identical two-story brick structures with two barracks on the second floor and two barracks on the first floor, e.g., four barracks per building. She pointed to the big "UB" sign on the center building and said,

"You have been assigned to barracks UB. Walk straight to barracks UB across the grass and red lined sidewalks. They are expecting you."

---

[5]https://prisonfinder.org/texas/federal-prison/fci-beaumont-low...Search Federal Prison Pictures of Beaumont Low...the only additions made are the labeling and location arrows

The worst part of entering prison is not knowing what to expect. I tried to calm myself by dwelling on the fact that people are sentenced to far longer than twenty-four months in prison and survive. And, I had spent time in military school and a small amount of time in the army, so I was used to discipline, and it was a "low" security prison as opposed to a medium or maximum-security prison. I must say, the walk across the yard with no one in sight carrying a small bag with my heart medication and a box with my CPAP and SoClean sterilizer units was perhaps the longest walk I have ever taken.

When I walked up to the door, I could see a female guard watching me through the glass window on the door (female guards in a male prison barracks surprised me). She unlocked and opened the door as I approached it and when I entered, she said,

"Keep walking straight back to the door ahead of you. You are assigned to the chicken coop; the first lower bunk on the left as you enter is yours." [6]

When I entered, I saw five double bunk beds that allowed ten men to sleep and live in a twenty foot by twenty-foot room with a window three-foot-wide by five-foot-high at one end with bars in front of the glass. There were seven men in the room either sitting on their bunk or in a plastic chair by their bunk. The bunk above me was empty. I sat my bag and box on the bunk that had a rolled-up mattress with two folded sheets, two blankets, a pillowcase. One of the men, Beau, who was sitting on the top bunk across the room from me said,

---

[6] chicken coop – the slang term for cell number 61 which is the only ten-man cell in the barracks. Each barracks has a chicken coop. It is usually where an inmate starts his sentence at Beaumont Low. I was in the chicken coop for six months before I moved to a three-man cell.

"Welcome to Beaumont."

I responded,

"Thanks, it's great to be here."

Everyone laughed and introduced themselves in a very cordial and pleasant manner. I made my bed as I remembered from the army and military school.

Over the next hour, each man introduced himself and said why he was in there and for how long. It occurred to me as they were telling me their story that eventually I would be expected to tell mine. All of the men in my cell were there due to crimes committed in one or more of these categories: (i) drugs, (ii) firearms or (iii) carrying illegals across the Mexican border to the United States. All were Hispanic except Beau who was Cajun. All of them, except Beau and me, had extensive gang-related tattoos. When it came my turn to tell why I was in Federal prison, they stopped me. One of them left and came back with Sam. Sam was white, about six feet tall with a shaved head and lots of tattoos. Sam was head of the "White Guys" in the barracks, including the white supremacists. Sam asked me,

"What ticket did you get that got you in here?"

My cellmates had told me that when it came to my turn, they would get Sam and I had to tell Sam and them why I was here, including showing them my "paper." Paper, I was told, was prison slang for the BOP (Bureau of Prisons) documents they give you upon entry to the prison. The documents show the beginning and end dates of your sentence, and it includes good behavior days so a 24-month sentence in my case showed September 25, 2020 as my out date — about 20 months total in BOP custody — with twelve months of probation afterward. It does not give specifics of what the charges are. Sam asked me straight out,

"Are you a SO (Sex Offender) or former prison guard, policeman or prosecuting attorney?"

I told him and my cellmates,

"No, I am not a Sex Offender, I took a plea deal to get dropped from a criminal conspiracy that would have given me about a sixty-month sentence. In return for pleading guilty to sending military explosives to a municipal landfill, I caught a twenty-four-month sentence at Beaumont Low."

Sam said,

"Can you prove what you just told us?"
I said,

"Yes, if you can search the internet, search "'Charles Ferris Callihan Explo Systems Minden, Louisiana' you will see my smiling face and the story I just told you."

Sam left and came back about four hours later and asked me,

"What is M6?"

I responded,

"You mean propellant?"

Sam said,

"Yes."

I said,

"M6 is a propellant charge for a 155m howitzer shell."

Sam slapped me on the back and said,

"Welcome brother, you're the man."

I had just been inducted into the White Guys at Beaumont Low. I subsequently learned there was a White Guys network that included all the barracks in the prison, including the medium, maximum, camp and SHU (pronounced "shoe").

SHU – Special Housing Unit – Is a two-man cell with a toilet, shower and sink and no privacy. You get one religious book, like the Quran or Bible, plus one other book. Meals are brought to your cell. Breakfast is like breakfast at the chow hall. Lunch is always bologna, bread and water (no condiments). Dinner is always whatever leftovers they had at the chow hall the day before, turned into either vegetable broth, chicken broth, or beef broth-based soup. It is not nearly as delicious as it sounds, I am told. You have one hour per day out of the cell in a yard like a cow pasture with no trail just a little grass, but just mud if it is wet. I never broke a rule to get to the SHU, but plenty of my acquaintances did.

Typical SHU Prison Cell

I also learned that the prison population was divided by race, gangs and culture and it was inmate run. Cartels are at the top and underneath them are gangs. Not only because of the number of members of the cartel (more than any other one gang), but because of their fierce loyalty to the cartel and its leader. Cartel members' loyalty is equivalent to Samurai loyalty to their master in feudal Japan. There is also a sub hierarchy of gangs. Gang hierarchy is based on the number of inmates in the gang in a particular barracks and also how aggressive they are. A gang in one barracks may be high in one barracks and lower in another based solely on the number of members in the barracks. The lowest of the inmate groups are the SO's (Sex Offenders). They do not have their own TV room and cannot watch TV except by standing outside the doorway of a particular group's TV room and watching through the door. SO's do this for sporting events in which they have wagered money. In UB barracks there are three TV rooms for these groups: White Guys, Hispanic, and African American. White supremacists were included in the White Guys because the Arian Brotherhood in our barracks only had four members and they did not want to separate themselves into a group separate from the White Guys (white men without gang affiliation) because they would be overwhelmed by the 60+ African Americans and 90+ Hispanics. Each of these groups were subdivided into gangs, but they were all united against the Arian Brotherhood. There was an understanding in place that if the Arian Brotherhood kept their racist rants out of hearing and did what Sam said with the White Guys they would be left alone. My perception is that those in the Arian Brotherhood had enough of a survival instinct to keep their mouths shut and go along with Sam's group.[7]

Lumped in with the SO's were former prison guards, policemen and prosecuting attorneys. Former prison guards, policemen and prosecuting attorneys are the ultimate outcasts in that even the SO's ignored them as much as possible. Within the SO's there are also subgroups. The top of the SO pecking order are pimps, below them are homosexuals and below them, just above former prison guards, policemen and prosecuting attorneys are pedophiles.

Included near the top of the SO's are inmates who are transsexuals and/or transvestites. Pretty

---

[7] cartel – an association of manufacturers and suppliers whose purpose is to restrict competition for a particular product or service, so prices remain relatively high. In this instance the products were heroin, cocaine and marijuana and the service was transporting illegal immigrants or human trafficking. In prison jargon, transportation of illegal immigrants for prostitution is known as "A Transportation and Labor Service."

transsexuals and/or transvestites have their own loyal following, including inmates who were not SO's but were in for decades or life. These inmates, called "lifers" or "long-timers" have made the best nest they can find from the material available (prison reality). If you were in the SO group in UB barracks your cells were all together at the end farthest away from the communal toilets, urinals, sinks and showers, e.g., the bathroom.

The cartel's cell block, The Shining Path, in UB barracks was on either side of the communal toilets, urinal, sinks and showers. There is an equivalent "pecking order" in each barracks whether it is the low, medium or maximum-security prison. In barracks UB, the top of the pecking order is a cartel called "The Shining Path." The Shining Path in UB barracks has about 50 members whose loyalty is very Samurai like to their master, Senõr González.[8]

The Shining Path is not the only cartel at Beaumont, but it is the most powerful in UB barracks and also in UA, SA and SB barracks. However, there are other cartels in place. The cartels I know are there are: Sinaloa, Medellin and Gulf. There are also gangs just below the cartels in pecking order and in some other barracks, they are at the top of the pecking order. Gangs prevalent at Beaumont in random order are: Hells Angels, Bandidos, Barrio Azteca, Los Mexicales, Paisas, and Sureños. All gang members have tattoos unique to

---

[8] The Shining Path began in the 1970's as a Maoist-Communist revolutionary group dedicated to overthrowing the Peruvian Government. They have since morphed into a cartel whose activities include "K and R" (Kidnap and Ransom). Their products are heroin, cocaine and marijuana. In addition, they conduct human trafficking with both prostitution and non-prostitution bound illegals on a large scale, e.g., continuously. Being a member of a cartel is an "in it for life" proposition. The cartel provides a steady income and protection from other cartels, gangs and government agents.

their gang and gang members watch out for one another.

During my time at Beaumont Low, I witnessed profound acts of kindness between members of a gang. For example, some gang members are in wheelchairs, paralyzed from the waist down due to gunshot wounds. Fellow gang members help them shower in the handicapped shower. That is, literally lifting them up in a firemen's carry, illustrated below, while another gang member positions his wheelchair under the water from the shower head. They leave the wheelchair bound man to wash himself. Then they hold him in the firemen's carry while another dries off the wheelchair and they place him back in it and help him get dressed. This is a daily occurrence. Also, three times a day, they make sure someone is assigned to push him to and from the chow hall for meals. One way to the chow is a quarter of mile – half a mile roundtrip. When it is raining, they make sure he has a raincoat and when they get back to the barracks, they dry his wheelchair off and make sure he always has dry towels.

Fireman's Carry

Once you learn the ropes, prison life is extremely low stress because you have very few decisions to make. You are awakened by loudspeaker at 6:00 AM with some version of, "Good Morning Beaumont Low" very loud. You stand in line to brush your teeth and shave. You stand in line to go to the toilet or take a shower. About 6:45AM, the loudspeaker says, "Chow!" However, that does not mean you get in line for chow, it just means the chow hall is ready to serve a meal. If your barracks is first, then the guard will yell, "In line UA side," which means you walk through double doors and go to the chow hall through the UA side barracks door. Or they would yell, "In line UB side," which means you walk straight out the UB barracks door accompanied by everyone from UA barracks. It is a quarter mile from the door of the barracks to the chow hall and you always walk counterclockwise, so everyone eventually gets a half mile walk to and from the chow hall three time a day if you eat every meal at the chow hall. Meals are optional, if you do not want to eat at the chow hall do not get in line. This process occurs for breakfast, lunch, and dinner every day.

I learned that four clothing irons and the top of a metal locker could make a really good grill. Also, that one clothing iron can be converted into a stinger. The heating element is removed and wired directly to a 110-volt electrical outlet bypassing the control. One lead is wired to the power source and the other is placed into a clean scrub bucket filled with tap water. The heating element is then placed into the bucket and the current between the heating element and the loose lead in the water will heat two gallons of water in about twenty minutes to boiling. When I first saw this in action I realized that if you put an insulator, such as a piece of wood, on one side of the heating element with its lead attached to the power source and attached the other wire to the back side of the insulator, a stronger current would pass between the leads through the water than with their current design and it would heat the water quicker. I mentioned this fact to the inmates using the stinger and forgot about it and about a week later three guys came into my cell with the "Charles Stinger." They had named it after me and it heated two gallons of water from room temperature to boiling in about five minutes instead of the usual twenty. As far as I know, several Charles Stingers are still in operation at Beaumont; I like that.

NOTE: If you try this at home, remember to not put your hand or anything metal with your hand attached into the water when it is being heated with a stinger because you will get a severe electrical shock, perhaps fatal. Also, post someone as a lookout because, while there may not be a prison guard where you live, there will probably be someone in your house that does not want the clothes iron dismantled and water heated in the manner, described above.

I did not think it possible, but you can actually use a stinger to heat two gallons of cooking oil or pure butter. I saw it done multiple times when frying burritos or making sopaipillas from pieces of tortillas. I thought it would catch fire and the potential for fire is present even if it does not catch fire. Remember, like all things you are not supposed to do, but do anyway, you have to be extra careful when you do it.

I figured out after about a week that not everyone ate every meal at the chow hall. I had sent my son-in-law enough money to wire $300 into my commissary account on the first day of each month for twenty-four months. You could spend up to $150 over a two-week period at the commissary which has dehydrated soup, tortillas, candy bars, peanut butter, chips, rice, packets of seasoned beef, chicken, mackerel, tuna and my favorite, fish steaks in

Louisiana hot sauce. Also, at the commissary are hygiene items, such as deodorant, toothpaste, toothbrushes, soap, shampoo and conditioner, and safety razors with shaving soap. There are even radios with headphones you can use to listen to the TV. The TV has no speaker, so everyone listens on headphones attached to the AM/FM radio. The TV signal, as I recall, is 88.7 on the FM dial. On Tuesdays, for example, you filled out your commissary sheet that has all the items available from the Commissary. There are boxes for each barracks at the entrance door to the chow hall and you put your commissary sheet into the box labeled with your barracks letters, UB for example. If you did not go to the chow hall, then you could give your commissary list to someone who puts it into the box for you.

Commissary day is the best day of the week for a lot of inmates. You get your food supply for the week and people who incur debts are able to pay them off. I learned the term $10 commissary which means someone has given you a list of items they want from the Commissary worth about $10. You put their list of items on your commissary sheet and when you get their items, along with yours, you pay or receive the items as appropriate.

Never in my musings about what prison life would be like did I envision that for $20 commissary every other week, I could have my shirts and pants ironed by another inmate. Also, if I bought a box of graham crackers and a box of vanilla wafers every week, and gave them to Jesus, I got a fresh piece of cheesecake, or whatever the cake of the evening was, delivered to my cell between 6:30 PM and 7:00 PM, every other night plus Saturday. For $10 commissary I could get my haircut in the bathroom. I could make an approximate appointment and he would come and get me when he was ready to cut my hair. For example, I would say to the barber, Rick,

"I would like to get my haircut tomorrow afternoon."

Rick would respond,

"Okay, what cell are you in?"

I would say,

"I am in the chicken coop."

Rick would come to my cell the next afternoon when he was ready to cut my hair and I would get my hair cut. You could also pay the equivalent of $10 in postage stamps, the other form of currency in the prison.

During the first week at Beaumont Low I learned how to make a visitors' list, how to send and receive emails and make telephone calls. Telephone calls are allowed from 5:00 PM until 9:00 PM, usually seven days a week, and you get 300 minutes per month. It seemed that most inmates used their minutes up early in the month so for a period of time toward the middle and end of the month they could not make any phone calls. Phone calls are only allowed to the people on your approved visitors' list. I called my wife every day and talked for up to 10 minutes each time. In this manner, I could call her throughout the month. The email system is up and running from 6:00 AM until 9:00 PM, usually seven days a week. It is not the usual email system. You could only send or receive emails from people on the approved visitors' list. Also, visitations are allowed on weekends, every other week. The week you are allowed to have visitors is based on the fifth digit of your BOP Inmate Number, whether it is even or odd; my number is 19865-035. The fifth number is "5" therefore, I could have visitors on the odd weekends of the month, e.g., the first, third and when available, the fifth weekend. If the weather was foggy enough that you could not see across the yard from the guards' viewing spots, they would cancel visitations. Also, during hurricanes, tropical storms or as punishment for a barracks or the prison in its entirety, they would cancel visitations. Punishments were always for fights among inmates, usually between gangs and sometimes within a gang where someone or group was trying to move up in the pecking order. It is substantially like wolf packs in how gang hierarchy is determined.

I also learned about the prison laundry. Upon arrival to Beaumont Low, you are issued uniforms: four shirts and three pairs of pants plus four pairs of boxer shorts, two long-sleeved and two short-sleeved tee shirts, fours pair of socks, one pair of tennis shoes, and one pair of boots. You are also issued two "slings." A sling is an elastic band with a clip so it can be made into a loop. On the sling is your name and Registration Number. Laundry in UB Barracks was Tuesdays and Thursdays. You used the two slings to attach underwear and socks to one sling and uniforms to the other. There were two bins stationed in the lobby area of the barracks on Tuesday and Thursday afternoons for two hours. You put your underwear in one bin and uniforms in the other. You got your clean laundry back on Wednesday and Friday and usually it was very damp. To complete the drying process, you had to lay your damp laundry out on your bunk, locker and wall that surrounded your cell. When the guards came by you had to get the laundry hung on the wall down because you were not supposed to have laundry on the wall and mean guards would take the laundry. We knew who the mean guards were so when they were on duty, there would be a lookout posted and he would yell,

"Mean guard on the prowl!"

Everyone would snatch their laundry down. I do not know if the mean guards did not like this, but if they did, they did nothing about it.

Where you rank, as an individual inmate, within inmate hierarchy is due mainly to the value the group in which you reside places on the skills you bring to the group. The highest skill in any group is the enforcer skill. Enforcers are big and strong enough and are willing enough to use violence, or the threat of violence toward whomever is not following inmate rules. Inmate rules have been developed to help prevent retribution by prison authorities or rival gangs or cartels. Inmate rules are few, but strictly enforced. I was told early on by Sam,

"The worst that can happen if you break guards' rules is, they put you in the SHU and/or take away your 'good time days.'[9] *If you break inmate rules, at a minimum you get beat up, and at worst you get maimed for life or killed outright."*

Inmate rules are few, just seven, but are strictly and swiftly enforced with no chance for appeal; inmate rules are:

i) Pay debts promptly.
ii) Do not bully anyone.
iii) Do not snitch on fellow inmates.
iv) Do not steal from your fellow inmates.
v) Do not cheat your fellow inmates.
vi) Do not take vengeance on a fellow inmate yourself. Instead, take it to the spokesman for your group. He will ensure, if your claim is deemed valid, that you receive adequate

---

[9] good time days — Days taken off your overall sentence for "good behavior" in prison jargon are called "good time days."

compensation. This rule ensures that rules are enforced in such a way that the group you are in, or the inmate population in general, are not punished because of your actions.

vii) Do not do anything that causes the group you are in, or the inmate population as a whole, to be punished because of your actions.

Most of the guards were nice. They looked the other way when inmates cooked food or heated water with the Charles Stinger. One particular female guard was a "Little Person." She would chat with you when she walked by your cell. Inmates were very protective of her. If an inmate, "sassed" her or did something inappropriate (like put semen on her office doorknob), they would be beaten to the point of having to go to the Medical Department. I never saw it occur during my time there, but I was told that it had occurred. On more than one occasion that I did witness, when this nice guard or other nice guards went on their rounds, they returned to their locked office to find a fresh piece of cheesecake on their desk to enjoy with a fresh cup of coffee. Their office door had been picked; the cheesecake placed in the middle of their desk along with coffee in a thermos mug. It was a game; I believe the guards enjoyed it as much as the inmates who did the deed.

The worst enemy to anyone in prison is what goes on in their mind. Every day, I saw inmates sitting in their bunks staring at the wall for hours at a time (I did my share of that too). The best friend to anyone in prison is also what goes on in their mind. Even staring at the wall can be a pleasant past time, if what you are thinking about is pleasant. I saw men who were sentenced to decades or even life in prison seem happy, and others, including me at times, sentenced to a few months and be devastatingly sad. The conclusion is that the length of one's sentence is not directly proportional to one's happiness while in prison. Just like on the outside, one's happiness depends on one's own mental attitude, along with how one behaves toward others. If you can make a circle of friends that you trust, they will help cheer you up when you are feeling down. If you can get something you can do every day that takes your mind off of where you are, that helps too. When I was standing in front of inmates, teaching algebra, chemistry, general science or social studies, my mind was on the subject being taught, and not on the fact that all of us were inmates in a federal prison.

A good example of being able to be happy while in prison occurred during the second month I was in prison. It was a Saturday and raining hard and it was supposed to rain all day which meant no rec yard, and walking to the Library without a decent raincoat meant sitting soaking wet while trying to read a book and about the time you got dry, you had to walk back in the rain. It was a half-mile roundtrip, so I concluded it was not worth the effort. All of us in the chicken coop were bored and then Riley said,

"Hey, let's make candy!"

I did not know you could make candy in a prison barracks and I had no idea how it was made. That did not matter, everyone else in the chicken coop did know how to make it, and they all got to work. One guy dug out his homemade screwdriver which did double duty as a shiv and started loosening the screws on the cover of the compressor at the bottom of the ice machine which is the coldest part at about 20°F. Another guy started cleaning off the top of his locker. Poncho asked me if I could spare a bag of coffee creamer and pointed out that Tuesday, commissary day, was only three days away.

I gave Poncho a new bag of creamer without asking why. Since carbonated soft drinks are not available, Kool Aid, for flavoring water is popular and you can get a box with 24 packets of Kool Aid at the Commissary. Poncho was separating packets of grape and cherry Kool Aid. Other guys were adding their Kool Aid packets to the pile. Another guy was heating water with the Charles Stinger in a Tupperware bowl.

When the water was not quite boiling, the packet of creamer I had donated was dumped into the water a little at a time while being stirred. Creamer was added until the consistency of cheesecake filling was obtained. Then, packets of grape Kool Aid were sprinkled into the filling and followed by the cherry Kool Aid packets. The resultant "paste" was spread about one-half inch thick in the bottom of a steel locker top/grill. When the paste was evenly spread, the locker top/grill was covered with a clean, clear trash bag and placed on top of the discharge side of the compressor at the bottom of the ice machine. The screws to the door of the compressor were replaced, but only finger tight. Picture, big, muscled prison inmates, all with gang tattoos all excited about making candy. In a couple of hours, the candy came out of the bottom of the ice machine and it was delicious taffy — a combination of grape and cherry. The taffy, with a cup of coffee, was a pleasant morning snack and enjoyed by everyone in the chicken coop on a rainy Saturday morning. *Happiness is where you find it.*

After three weeks of living life in prison I was bored out of my mind. So, I decided to get a job. On the outside I had moved from part time, teaching Process Technology[10] with a full-time chemical

---

[10] Process Technology – a two-year bachelor's degree that is specialized to qualify you to be an operator in a chemical plant or refinery

engineering job to being a full-time professor and Process Technology Department Chairman and a part time chemical engineering consultancy. I figured I could teach in the GED (General Education Diploma) program. All inmates who wanted a job anywhere in the prison had to have at least a GED, so the program had a waiting list of inmates (students) and a shortage of qualified teachers.

I walked to the Education Department at education work call and met with the GED department head. He pulled up my file on his computer, and said,

"Wow, when can you start? The job pays $45.63 a month directly into your commissary account."

He told me he had never seen someone with BS and MS degrees in chemical engineering, an MBA, who was a College Department Chairman, and Professor who was also a member of MENSA, as an inmate in a federal prison. I felt as special as when on my first day in prison I was informed of which sidewalks I could use, which direction on the sidewalks I could walk, and on what side of the sidewalk I could walk. I said,

"I can start now, if you want."

He walked me two doors down and into the classroom that would be my home almost the entire time at Beaumont Low, and introduced me to the inmate instructor who was teaching algebra whose name was Carlos. Carlos is Charles in Spanish I learned that day.

Carlos had a liberal arts degree from Tulane University in New Orleans and was teaching algebra because there was no one else as remotely qualified as he was to teach algebra. I sat in the back of the room for the rest of the first class and listened and watched as he taught. I sat halfway through the second class and after the second-class break, I took over and never relinquished the position until one month prior to leaving when they found a mechanical engineer who had ended up at Beaumont Low to take over from me. The teaching week was Monday through Friday from 7:30 AM until 11:30 AM when we broke for lunch, and then from 12:30 PM until 3:30 PM when the day ended. I taught three classes in the morning and two classes in the afternoon. The last hour of the day was tutoring students in any subject they wanted and students from the morning class who needed tutoring in algebra or chemistry or any other subject in the GED program could show up at 2:30 PM and I would help them with it. I taught or tutored in every subject in the GED curriculum except English as a second language because I do not speak Spanish.

Prison life, and its culture, are the opposite of life on the outside. Before I started teaching, found the Library, and started having my two sisters send me books on a regular basis, I hung out in the White Guys TV room or laid in my bunk and daydreamed about not being at Beaumont Low. The TV channels watched were not decided by a majority because preference was given (rightly so) to inmates who were lifers, or who had been in the barracks a longtime. Sam was the spokesman for the White Guys, so he got preference. Harold, one of my cellmates, also got preference because he had been in the barracks for a long time and had a long time to go. Since Sam and Harold liked the same TV programs, there were no arguments. The only time I changed the channel on the TV is when someone else, like Sam or Harold, asked me to change the channel since my assigned chair was right in front of the TV, an honored place. Being the barracks medic meant not having to stand in line in the bathroom, and also I had a front row seat in the TV room anytime I wanted it.[11] If someone was in "my chair" when I came in, they would move somewhere else so I could sit in it. This was another situation I had never imagined would occur to me during my time in prison at Beaumont Low.

An example of prison life and its culture being the opposite of the outside world are programs watched on TV. There are three TV series watched constantly, and the only deviation is if there is a sports event where betting on the outcome is prevalent. The three series are Swamp People, Kick Boxing and any detailed story or documentary about crime, such as Dangerous Women and I Almost Got Away with It.

The crime documentaries would have an ongoing discussion during the program by inmates on what they should or could have done to have gotten away with it. Or, how stupid a particular move was on the part of the criminal that got him caught. In one instance, the story involved a criminal who had served time in the federal prison near Florence, Colorado.[12] The TV program showed a picture of the prison and one of the inmates in the TV room yelled,

"I spent four years there!"

Everyone gave him a round of applause and he stood up and took a bow.

One of the true crime documentaries on TV one day when I did not have anything worthwhile to read was a documentary about life in Sing Sing

---

[11] Barracks Medic — How I got to be the barracks medic is described later in detail.

[12]USP Florence which includes a camp is in Fremont County near Florence, Colorado. It is also called "Alcatraz of the Rockies" and "Supermax."

Prison.[13] The prison barracks looked surprisingly like the barracks at Beaumont Low and the cells were the same as ours in Beaumont Low but they had barred doors and bars that went to the ceiling above the seven foot high cinder block walls. In Beaumont Low, there are no bars above the seven-foot cinder block walls and no doors at the entrance to the cells. I am told Beaumont Medium is like Beaumont Low, but with bars like I saw in the Sing Sing documentary. The inmates looked like us but had white uniforms while ours was khaki.

I made the mistake of saying to the group in the TV room,

"I can't believe we're sitting here as inmates in prison watching a TV documentary about inmates in prison. If you want to see inmates in prison, go sit in the hallway. I find this very ironic."[14]

Someone asked me,
"Hey! What's 'ironic' mean?"

I had to define what ironic is and site examples, like getting caught for a crime, getting out, repeating the same crime, and getting caught again, and being surprised you were caught even though you were doing the same thing that got you caught the first time. One of the inmates said,

"I didn't know I as acting ironically, and that is why I got caught a second and a third time. I'm in here for life now, so I don't have to worry about acting ironically anymore."

---

[13] Sing Sing Prison — A New York State Prison located at 354 Hunter Street — Ossining, NY 10562
[14] ironic — happening in the opposite way to what is expected, and typically causing wry amusement because of this

I had to agree with him. And I made a silent vow never to comment on another TV program no matter how much it reeked of "irony."

The TV program, Swamp People, involves mostly Cajon men in shallow draft boats going after alligators. The plot is simple, set the bait, go back and look, and if the line is taught, pull the alligator close to the boat, shoot it in the head at pointblank range, pull it into the boat and go on to the next baited line and do it again. If you have seen one alligator shot in the head at close range, you essentially have seen them all. However, to the inmates in the White Guys TV room, that plot never gets old. There are actually a few Cajun women who are couples, big scary girls, that also bait the hook, pull the alligator close to the boat, shoot it in the head and pull it into the boat, etc. These women have a loyal fan base in the federal prison system. I suspect they also get fan mail from the inmates, but this is just my supposition.

In the crime documentary shows, I witnessed arguments between inmates that almost came to blows because one of the inmates thought he could have gotten away with it one way and another inmate thought it should have been another way. It was actually more amusing and entertaining to watch and listen to the inmates' interactions with one another during the TV programs than the program itself. I gradually stopped watching TV when I got my job teaching/tutoring in the GED program, found the Library and started receiving books from my sisters on a regular basis.

Kick Boxing, especially women's kick boxing, is also an extremely popular TV program in prison. Before prison, I did not know that women's Kick Boxing even existed. The women in Kick Boxing also have a loyal fan base in the federal prison system, probably including fan mail, I am sure.

Days seemed to pass quickly in prison. During the day, it sometimes seemed to be dragging by, but then it was 9:15 PM and for me, it was time to get ready for bed; my day was over. Pretty soon, another week would be over and so on. Days really did drag over holidays. I spent one Wife's Birthday, my birthday, Thanksgiving, Christmas and New Years in prison and two July Fourths and two Easters as wells as two Wedding Anniversaries. The chow hall could produce really good meals, as good as you could get at a Wyatt's Cafeteria for example. Why they did not do that every day is a mystery to me. However, on Thanksgiving Day and Christmas it would be a traditional turkey dinner with all the trimmings, including your choice of vanilla, strawberry or chocolate ice cream, each in its own little carton with a wooden spoon. The ice cream was like I remembered getting in grade school in the 1950's. Easter was similar only it was ham instead of turkey, but the ice cream was there in the carton with the little wooden spoon. I remember during our Christmas dinner the intercom was playing Christmas songs. I thought, I am sad because I am in here for Christmas, but it is the only Christmas I will spend in here. The guy sitting next to me was a lifer and this is his Christmas experience for the rest of his life, and he is in his late twenties. Now, that is sad!

An event bigger even than Christmas in prison is Super Bowl Sunday. On Super Bowl Sunday, when you go to lunch chow, on the way out they hand you a sack dinner and a bottled water. The Super Bowl is on TV by dinner time and no one would want to go to dinner chow (even the guards) during the Super Bowl, so we all got a sack dinner. The sack dinner contained, four pieces of sandwich bread, two slices of salami, enough peanut butter for two sandwiches, a small bag of potato chips, a small bag of Oreo cookies, a Butternut candy bar, a packet of mustard, a packet of grape jelly, and a packet of mayonnaise. I traded the peanut butter and jelly for more salami and mayonnaise.

There were decorations for Thanksgiving, Christmas, Halloween and Easter. The decorations for all holidays are stored in the mop closet on the top couple of shelves. I found it both amusing and fascinating that the only inmates who put up, took down and cared for the decorations were the transvestites and transsexuals. I pointed that out one day around Christmas to the guys in the TV room by saying,

"If it weren't for the transvestites and transsexuals, there would be no Christmas decorations or Thanksgiving, Halloween, etc... aren't you glad they are in here with us?"

They all looked at me weird, said nothing and went back to watching TV. Sometimes, I said things just to see their reaction; sometimes I regretted it.

One of the new cellmates in the chicken coop when I was still in the chicken coop saw one of the prettier transsexuals walk into the bathroom in front of him. He came back to the chicken coop and said,

"I didn't know there were men who thought they were women in here. I thought they sent them to a special place."

I said,

"They do send them to a special place. And they sent you there too!"

He thought for a few of seconds and laughing said,

"Damned if they didn't."

The essence of successfully integrating into prison life is the knowledge that the culture is based on "Platoon Mentality." I had already learned this culture in military school and the army, so it was easy for me to recognize. In a Platoon Mentality culture, everyone has a place and a skill that is useful to the group. There are only two aspects to Platoon Mentality:

i) no one is going to help us, but us, and
ii) everyone is against us, who is not us.

In this culture, it is easy to see why a "snitch" or a "thief" within the platoon is considered worse than a SO, former prison guard or prosecuting attorney. At least, SO's, prison guards and prosecuting attorneys are tolerated in the barracks. They are not attacked on sight regardless of the consequences. Not so with a snitch or a thief. Inmates who are judged and found guilty by their fellow inmates of either of these crimes, if they have the opportunity, go to the guard and request to be sent to the SHU because they legitimately fear for their lives.

Chapter V
You Can't Make This Stuff Up

Finally, something to look forward to Monday through Friday – teaching and tutoring. Education work call is at 7:30 AM, ± 10 minutes. You must hang out on the UA side and wait for the guard to come out of his or her office and unlock the door. You walk counterclockwise until you get to the sidewalk that is marked with a yellow stripe that goes to Education, Legal, Library, Psychology, and Chapel. You also have to walk on the right half of the sidewalk no more than three abreast. There is that feeling special again. I had that special feeling every morning I had to "walk this way."

My third day I witnessed the first of many "you can't make this stuff up" moments. These moments made prison life more bearable besides giving me worthwhile material to write in this book. I found out later the guy's name was Raoul and he was from Puerto Rico. Raoul was maybe five feet tall at most, but very muscular like a gymnast, and he had dreadlocks down his back almost to his waist. Raoul lives in barracks VA, the second floor of the building on the left if you are facing the middle building where UA and UB barracks are located. To get to the second floor there is a stairway with an intermediate landing about ten feet above grade. Inmates I am walking along with are all looking at VA barracks and pointing at the landing where Raoul is balanced on the top rail about fourteen feet above the ground. He has his arms out for balance like he is on a cross; his eyes are closed, and he is breathing deeply. He leans forward and falls face first toward the ground, does one complete forward somersault in mid-air, lands on his feet and rolls, gets up and starts to walk on the sidewalk like everyone else.

Raoul was one of my students and he exited VA barracks every time in this manner. I, and most everyone else, at mealtimes and at Education work call would always look to see if Raoul were going to perform. Raoul was a good student. His problem in learning was not lack of comprehension of algebra or science; it was his lack of understanding of written English. He could speak English, but not read it. I got him enrolled in English as a Second Language and his comprehension of algebra, chemistry, general science and social studies improved continuously during my tenure, and he passed his GED exam my final week as a teacher/tutor in the GED program.

Raoul's best performance was about a month later during the noon chow call. He made his exit from VA barracks in the usual manner. Inmates applauded his building exit routine as usual and I even saw some of the guards applaud. It was a Thursday and I always had lunch at the chow hall on Thursday's because it was baked chicken, mashed sweet potatoes, green beans and an apple; the best lunch of the week to me. Anyway, Raoul had made his exit as usual and garnered the applause and then halfway to the chow hall he walks off the sidewalk onto the grass which is a major rule break.

You never, ever walk on the grass because you will spend a week in the SHU, and you will have your khaki uniforms confiscated and replaced with bright yellow shirts and pants. A bright yellow uniform identifies you as a trouble-maker to the guards and the guards harass you like trashing your cell, e.g., throwing your bedding and all of your possessions in the middle of the floor, or making you mow the twenty acre yard in the hot sun without a hat using a hand push mower. Everyone stops and looks at Raoul who is just standing about thirty feet off the sidewalk on the grass. The guards have noticed too. Raoul, very slowly, puts his hands with his index fingers pointing on the left and right side of his head like the horns on a bull. Then, very slowly, he starts pawing the grass like a bull who is getting ready to charge. He picks out Sidney, the biggest, meanest guard in the yard at the time and starts running straight for him with his head down and his index fingers on each side of his head just like a bull. Of course, when he reaches Sidney, Sidney side steps him, slams him to the ground and puts handcuffs on him and leads him away to the SHU amidst thunderous applause from every inmate in the yard and some of the guards. Raoul spent a week in the SHU, and when he got out, he had to wear the yellow uniform for a week, but I found out no guards harassed him during his yellow uniform week, not even Sydney.

Just after Raoul got back from the SHU, I was standing in line at the Commissary. It was UB barrack's turn, a Tuesday, about 10:30 AM. It had been an ordinary day up to that point, and then I saw him. An inmate from another barracks. A huge in shape African American with long dreadlocks (dreadlocks are quite common on African American inmates at Beaumont Low) had started running on the grass in the Yard! At first, the guards yelled at him, and he responded by smiling, waving at them and continuing to run on the grass. Then, six guards tried to corner him, but he easily outran, and side stepped them. Picture an NFL running back in broken field running against six out of shape men and women trying to catch him. It was no contest. He even let a female guard get close enough to touch him, but then ran away from her. Every inmate in the commissary line was now yelling and cheering for him. I was smiling, but otherwise trying to maintain my casual observer of human behavior attitude. He ran close to the commissary line where the 175 of us from UB barracks were standing in line and asked, "What time is it?" We yelled 10:50 AM." He yelled back, "I started at 10:30 and will try to keep going until 11:30." Of course, we yelled encouragement to him, including me, and continued to cheer and clap every time he let a guard get close to him and then would run away. About 11:30, he laid down in the middle of the yard and put his hands behind him like he was wearing handcuffs.

Two guards ran up to him and put hand cuffs on him, helped him up, and started walking him toward the SHU. He said something to the guards that made them stop and one of the guards put his hand down the front of his gym shorts and came out with a brown envelope. I found out later, it was a note to the warden for all of Beaumont's prisons. I also found out that an inmate can send a message through any guard to the warden and if the guard is found to not have passed it on to the warden, the guard can lose his job and pension. The guards, having been laughed at by all of us, cancelled commissary for us for the week and sent us back to the barracks. This decision was appealed by a note to the warden, and we got to go to commissary two days later. The guy spent a week in the SHU, and he was let out four days before he was scheduled to go to the halfway house. He was given the honorary name of "Yard Runner" by the inmates and we bowed to him and shook his hand at every opportunity for his remaining four days at Beaumont Low. The note he had written to the warden, said:

"I am within four weeks of my halfway house date and have never broken any rule in the three and one-half years I have been at Beaumont Low. I got my GED here and became certified in auto mechanics at the prison Votech School. I ran in the Yard for an hour to make sure this note gets to you. Guards in VA barracks trash inmates' cells for no reason three or four nights a week. It started when an inmate made a pass at a female guard, and she has been re-assigned to another prison. The inmate who made the pass spent a month in the SHU and is now back and

has caused no additional problems. Trashing of inmates' lockers started just after he made the pass and has not stopped even though no other rules have been broken. Please stop this practice!"

The note worked in that inmates' cells in VA barracks immediately stopped being trashed.

Smuggling is an art form in prison, at least at Beaumont Low. It was a sought-after skill. Inmates who could obtain food from the chow hall were held in high regard. Other items were drill bits from the prison shop because they were the best items to make into shivs. Inmates made a job of being given an item to obtain and then getting it smuggled into the barracks. Tommy was one of the best. He was a cellmate of mine for a while in the chicken coop. Tommy had the bunk above me. He was six feet two inches tall and weighed 320 pounds. His uniform was baggy, XXXL, so he could smuggle food from the chow hall where he worked. Tommy set the record for smuggling hard boiled eggs. He smuggled two dozen hard boiled eggs out of the chow hall in his socks. I was there to witness it. Knowing that if an inmate smuggles something out of the chow hall, they have to pay others who help them, I asked Tommy,

"How many more eggs did you have to get in order to walk out with two dozen?"

Tommy said,

"I didn't have to get anymore because the guys I worked with told me that was too many and I'd get caught. They said, 'If you can smuggle two dozen eggs out in your socks, we want to see that, and we don't need any payment.'"

Tommy's smuggling ability became legendary, and he started taking orders for specific food items, and as far as I know, he always delivered. That morning he ate three of the eggs he smuggled out and sold the rest for two stamps each.

One of the most colorful characters I met, and the only inmate I personally saw get tasered, is Victor. Victor has a likeness of President Trump's head tattooed on the right side of his shaved head above his hairline, if he ever let his hair grow. The tasering occurred during a Thursday lunch in the chow hall at the point where inmates pick up their tray of food at the end of the serving counter. Inmates can go through the line as many times as they want, but they must go to the end of the line and not cut in line. Victor wanted two trays so he would not have to go back through the line. Victor had been in Beaumont for about two years and he knew the rule, "One inmate, one tray" each time you go through the line. Why Victor on this particular day, even though it was a good lunch, decided to break the rule, I do not know why, and I suspect, neither does Victor.

The guard at the end of the lunch chow line was African American, female and about five feet tall. Victor is six feet tall and weighs about two hundred fifty pounds. Victor bent down, awfully close to the guard's face and said, "I'm taking two trays." The guard backed up three steps and tasered him without warning. Victor dropped the tray he had and began to convulse on the floor. Six other guards came running, the chow lunch line was halted in place which means you just stand where you are. Two other guards arrived in about five minutes with a wheeled stretcher and took Victor away, first to Medical and then to the SHU. I found out later from another inmate, Victor was serving twenty years in federal prison for mailing Ricin laced letters to Democratic members of congress. No one was injured from the mailing, but the intent was clearly there. *Perhaps Victor has mental issues, like he is deranged, and should not be in the general population of any prison?*

After about a month, I stopped eating at the chow hall except for Thursday lunch. From the Commissary I got oatmeal for breakfast and I paid Herald (more about Herald later) a packet of regular coffee weekly from the Commissary. In return, Herald would smuggle to me from the chow hall four pieces of bread and two apples when he could which was almost daily. I had tuna, mackerel, peanut butter, mustard, and mayonnaise from the Commissary as well as club crackers and that was usually lunch using the bread I got from Herald and the crackers plus the apples. Dinner would either be dehydrated soup made with water from the hot water tap,[15] or a sandwich made with bread or crackers and tuna or mackerel. My favorite dinner was noodles from a packet of dehydrated soup with the broth poured off and fish steaks stirred in with the noodles (big pieces of some kind of fish) with Louisiana hot sauce – heavenly bliss with every mouthful is what I was told. It did not quite live up to that standard, but I knew it was better than whatever was being served in the chow hall for dinner.

The one time during my stay at Beaumont Low where I had to urinate in a cup for a drug and alcohol test occurred during my first month of imprisonment. Kenneth, a fellow chicken coop celli, had a K2 pipe (synthetic marijuana) and it had fallen out of his pocket and onto his bunk so that when he got up it stayed in the middle of his bunk. Every

---

[15] hot water tap – water just below boiling from a faucet next to the ice machine. There were no microwaves, but with this hot water you can have instant coffee with non-dairy coffee creamer and dehydrated soup.

night about 9:00 PM there was count. When they announced count, you had to get up and stand by your bunk until you were counted by two guards who came into the cell and physically counted you. When they announced count, they always started with the chicken coop so there was no time between when they announced count and when the guards walked into the chicken coop to count. Therefore, Kenneth's pipe was still in the middle of his bunk when the guards came in. The policy is rather than just to just test the guy who had evidence of K2 use, all the inmates in the cell are tested. So, we were all marched to the Lieutenant's office where there is a toilet without a privacy screen around it for inmates to collect a urine sample while a guard, male or female, watches you urinate, including me.

When we got back to the cell, Anthony and Gerard had a "talk" with Kenneth that involved slugging Kenneth in the stomach and pushing him up against the wall because he had brought all of us under suspension of K2 use. Kenneth was defiant and said to back off or "fight to the death." The phrase "fight to the death" is taken literally at Beaumont and Anthony and Gerard did back off. Nothing more was said about the incident.[16]

All went along as normal after the confrontation with Kenneth. Then a couple of days later, when Kenneth opened his locker, he found everything in his locker was just as he had left it the last time he had opened it, including his stash of K2,

---

[16]Each inmate, upon arrival, is issued a combination lock for their locker. It is identical to the combination lock used on high school lockers. It is a common skill in prison, to be able to pick locks. A simple combination lock like the one we were all issued can be opened inside of ten seconds. I actually learned this skill while in prison. It is always good to pick up bits of knowledge at every opportunity.

except the jar that held the K2 was also filled to the brim with urine. Kenneth looked very startled and angry and cast his eyes about the cell and was met with the same stare by his fellow inmates. Kenneth walked out with his K2-urine filled jar and came back empty handed and there was never a word said about it from anyone from that day on. Kenneth did not cause any more problems for the chicken coop during the remainder of his time there. I was told of other instances when an inmate is causing problems for this fellow cellmates. The offending inmate, when he opens his locker, finds all of his clothes soaked with urine. It is a warning you get, if you do not heed the urine warning, you then get a night visit or shower visit by the enforcers.

Technology always has a good and a bad side. For example, when nuclear power first appeared, it was heralded as the answer to cheap and safe electricity for everyone. Of course, the other side of nuclear power is nuclear weapons, potentially ending all of humanity. Drone technology, though certainly not as earth shattering as nuclear power, also has its good and bad side. And, like most issues that have a good and bad side, what is "good" and what is "bad" depends on which side you are on. The good side of drone technology is potentially, cheap and secure delivery of medicine to remote areas and to housebound people. The bad side is that it can be used to spy on people. In a prison environment, you can use drones to deliver contraband.

A prison drone delivery system starts with a cell phone delivered by a guard who has been bribed to get the cell phone to a particular inmate, or to place the cell phone under the trash bin nearest to the entrance/exit doors at a particular time and date. The cell phone has been pre-programmed with software that allows the drone to be controlled when it is within range. Outside the prison, the package of cell phones, cigarettes, K2, and/or pornography on a stick file is attached to the drone. The outside person drives to a point near the prison but concealed which is easy to do at Beaumont because the prison is surrounded by forest.

The drone is piloted by the outside person at a pre-arranged date and time on a vector toward and into the prison grounds at a height of no less than 100 yards. The height is important because at night at heights above 100 yards, the drone cannot be seen or heard by the casual observer. The inmate with the pre-programmed cell phone will automatically get a signal that the drone is on its way. The drone appears on the cell phone and with a push of a button on the cell phone, the inmate is now the drone pilot. The drone is flown to a point where the guards do not normally look, like the trash roll off bins at the back of the chow hall. The drone hovers above the bins and is lowered to six feet above the ground, and the contraband package is released.

The drone is then raised to a height a little above 100 yards and flown back along the same vector as it entered the prison. At a point near the fence line, the outside person takes over piloting the drone. The next morning, an inmate whose job is to dump smaller containers of trash into the roll off bins behind the chow hall, retrieves the contraband package and passes it to someone who is good at smuggling. That is, good at getting items from the chow hall to the barracks without being caught. This scenario is repeated as often as the supply and demand chain requires. A cell phone sells for about $1500 in prison. Money is wired from and to the applicable accounts by outside support people, identical to how bets are paid over sporting events.

One of the oddities of prison is that internet access could be jammed by prison authorities. If the internet were not available inside the prison because of jamming, there would be no market for illicit cell phones. In addition, drones could not be controlled via cell phone in the manner, described above. Why do not prison authorities just jam internet signals? When I asked that question of my fellow inmate, while the guy was piloting the drone toward the back of the chow hall, the answer genuinely surprised me. The answer is that there is a law that prohibits governmental entities from jamming public access to the internet. The law was passed with the well-meaning intention of prohibiting the government from censoring free speech by its citizens. We, in the United States, do not want our government to have the power of censorship like the governments of say China and Iran. Of course, the law could be amended to allow prison authorities to jam the internet, but apparently it is not that important. The resultant loophole in the law allows drone technology to deliver contraband to inmates in prison and it is most appreciated by the inmates who use the contraband to increase the quality of their lives while in prison.

Prior to drone technology, the method of contraband delivery depended on bribing guards, or having an outside person drive to a point along the fence line outside the prison and literally throw the contraband package over the barbed wire fence or wall. The package would later be retrieved by inmates or even a guard that had been bribed. One of the inmates I talked to said when he was in another prison in California, he had his girlfriend throw a contraband package over the fence at a point where the prison boundary fence bordered a public road on the outside and a jogging trail on the inside. The intent was that the next morning he would retrieve the package laying on the ground near the fence line and jogging trail. However, the execution of the plan did not go as planned. The girlfriend, when she threw the contraband package over the fence, managed to snag it in the concertina wire on the top of the fence.

Prison Fence Line

Nothing looks more like a contraband package than a small brown paper wrapped box snagged in concertina wire on a prison fence. Of course, the guards found the package which contained a dozen cell phones. They traced the cell phones to where they were bought and who bought them. They determined the girl that bought them was the same girl as on the inmate's approved visitor list. That episode got her eighteen months in prison and two years' probation. It also ended their relationship. The inmate lost Commissary and email privileges for six months and loss of his good behavior days which was about six months.

Something that I could not imagine, or that anyone else could imagine, if they were not an inmate in prison, is the guard dynamic within the guard community. There are several couples, both heterosexual and lesbian, where they are both guards and are on the same shift but assigned to different barracks. No guard stays for longer than a week in any one barracks and then you do not see them again for a month or six weeks in the same barracks, but you see them in the yard or in the chow hall.

One evening, about two hours after dinner, I heard two people yelling at each other near the guard's office. Two people yelling at each other is pretty common in a prison barracks. Sometimes I thought people were fighting and yelling at the same time and when I checked, it was everyone yelling and pounding chairs and tables while starring at the TV because their favorite team they were watching on TV was either doing really well, or not so well. However, in this instance, it seemed really strange because the two voices sounded definitely female. Even the transvestites and transsexuals did not sound that female.

I walked from my cell down the hall and looked tentatively around the corner, and I saw about a dozen inmates surrounding two female guards, and the two female guards were yelling at each other about some guy they were both dating. One of the guards did not want the other guard to go out with him and that guard thought she had every right to go out with him since he had asked her out. One of the inmates who was watching the argument turned to me and said,

"If they come to blows, should we try to separate them?"

I said,

"Absolutely not, you will end up in the SHU. If they come to blows, everyone run back to their cells and leave them to work it out on their own!"

Word was quickly past from inmate to inmate and several of them looked at me and gave me the "thumbs up" gesture. Fortunately, they did not come to blows, but it was close, and both had clubs and pepper spray so it could have been bad. It was, however, quite amusing and was talked about for months, and probably still is being reminisced about on quiet evenings in the barracks when nothing else is going on.

There is a constant passive aggressive dynamic occurring between inmates and prison guards and other prison authorities. Inmates, at the slightest provocation, will violate a rule, especially if they know they can get away with it. The first example of this that I noticed was when exiting the chow hall, I saw inmates putting slices of sandwich bread in their pants pockets. Then, on the way back to their barracks they would take the piece of bread out of their pockets, break off pieces and throw the pieces on the grass for the sea gulls to eat. There were signs along the path that stated, "DO NOT FEED THE BIRDS." I asked an inmate who was feeding the birds, why he and a lot of others were feeding the birds. He said,

"The sea gulls have always been here, and no one ever fed them until they put the 'DO NOT FEED THE BIRDS' signs up. The signs made it worthwhile to feed the birds. I'll give you a piece of bread and you can feed the birds if you want."

Of course, I said,

"Yes, please. I would like to feed the birds."

I must admit, it was a satisfying feeling to feed the birds in front of the "DO NOT FEED THE BIRDS" sign.

One morning, soon after I had met Harold, who was to become one of my closest friends and cellmate, Harold said to me about 6:15 AM one morning,

"Get your coat on. I'm going to show you how to behave like a convict."

At 6:30 AM the loudspeaker announcement called for diabetics to go to medical so they could get their insulin shots. I stood by Harold and when the diabetic inmates started walking out of the barracks, Harold and I mingled with them and walked out with them. When we got to medical, we stood in the middle of the line and let the real diabetics go in front of us. When a diabetic inmate got his shot, he was free to walk out of medical and go to the chow hall for breakfast. When three or four inmates who had gotten their shots started walking toward the chow hall, Harold and I fell in behind them and walked with them to the chow hall. Harold and I went through the chow line, got our breakfasts, ate at our leisure and then walked back to the barracks knowing we had violated the rules, gotten away with it and had a good breakfast without having to stand in line any time at all. Harold turned to me when we entered the barracks and said,
"Now, don't you feel better about yourself?"

I said,

"Yes, I do, it was exciting and pleasant, all at the same time."

Harold said,

"Now you have begun to think like a convict; keep it up."

Almost every day I was surprised in prison either by acts of kindness toward one another or acts of depravity toward one another. Both of these extremes of human behavior were largely ignored by everyone, including me. I ignored them because I did not know what to do in either case and I did not want to call attention to myself in either instance. I could site numerous examples, but I provide three here, so you get the idea of what one is faced with every day in prison — the good, the bad, and the depraved.

The Good — I walked into the barracks Library to look for a book one Wednesday evening about 8:00 PM and sitting around the table that had been moved to the far corner of the Library (it usually sat in the middle of the Library), were four members of the Sureños gang. I could tell by their tattoos...

Sureños

Bandidos

Shining Path

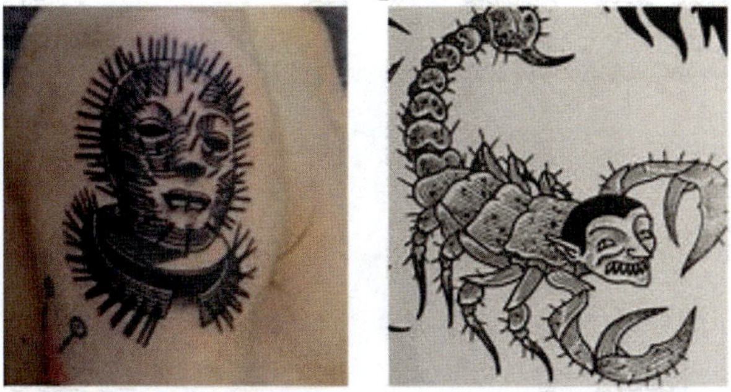

Barrio Azteca

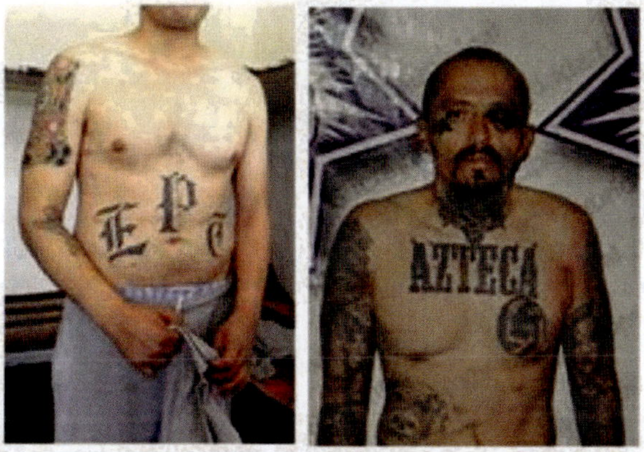

Arian Brotherhood

Los Mexicales

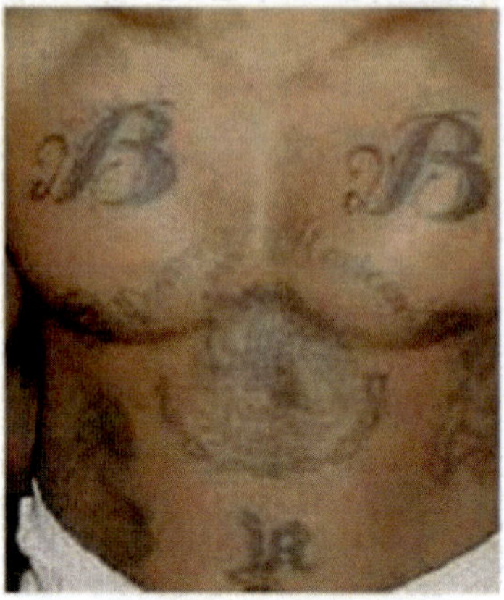

Paisas

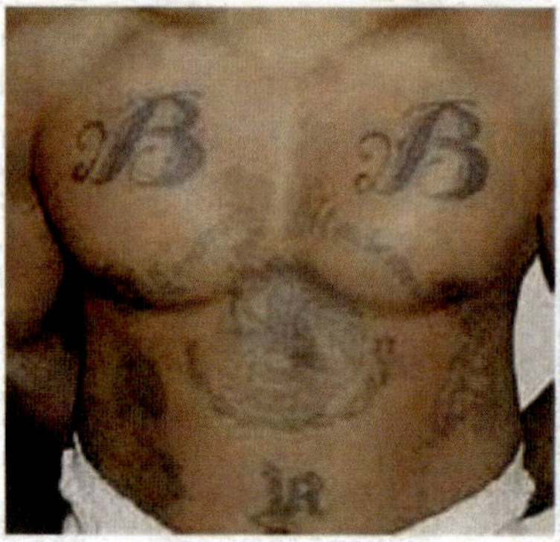

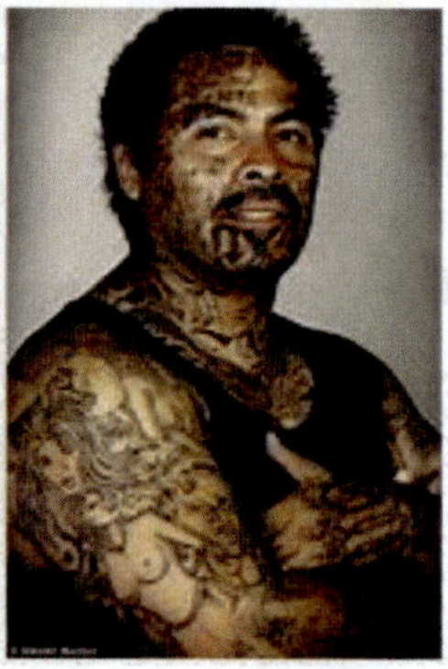

Hells Angels

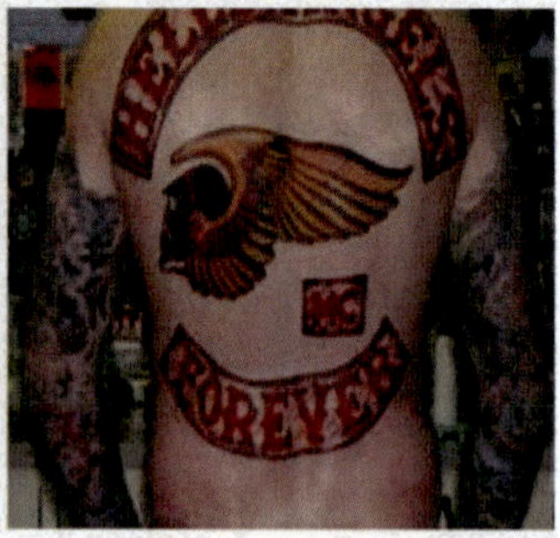

I initially thought, "I wonder what they are cooking up?" However, as I was leaving, I realized each man had a Bible in front of him in Spanish. They all had their Bibles open to the Gospel of Luke ("Evangelio de Lucas" in Spanish), and they were in the middle of a Bible study in Spanish. *Who knew?*

The Bad — A couple of times a month, a SO, while walking to or from the bathroom through The Shining Path section of the barracks, would be punched and verbally abused. Sometimes their head would be pressed hard against the cinder block wall and pushed along it until their face and/or scalp were scraped and bleeding. I could treat them as the barracks medic if they requested treatment. Most of the time they did not request anything. I remember only two occasions when treatment was requested. The SO's who received this treatment seemed unaffected by it. It is as if they had become accustomed to it and it was a normal part of life in prison.

The Depraved — I was awakened early one morning, about 2:00 AM by two inmates. They were in panic mode because they, along with another inmate, had been smoking K2 in the shower area of the bathroom. The other inmate they had just left on the floor in convulsions. I grabbed my first aid kit and ran into the shower area to find the inmate who had been in convulsions sitting up next to the wall. He had vomited down his tee shirt. He had a smile on his face and said,

"That's the best K2 I've ever had. Give me a minute and I'll be ready for more."

I said to the other two inmates,

"If you charge him up again tonight and he convulses again. Get the guard, not me."

I went back to my cell and went to sleep.

Life in the ten-man cell (chicken coop) was okay, but I needed to find a place in a three-man cell. In order to get “invited” to be the third man in a three-man cell you had to cultivate a friendship with at least one of the inmates in the cell. If you did not obtain an invitation to a three-man cell after about six months, they would assign you a cell and you might not get cellmates that you wanted to live with. There was no danger for me of being placed in an SO’s cell because I was with Sam and the White Guys. It would be a cell with white guys, but some of them were sketchy. I realized early on in prison that some of my fellow inmates were in prison for reasons like no awareness of the consequences of their actions and no concept of what responsibility and accountability mean. Therefore, I cultivated a friendship with Harold, the guy who brought me bread and apples and taught me how to behave like a convict, and Ricardo who had been in the bunk above me for a couple of weeks before he moved in with Harold and José. The reason I was stuck in the ten-man cell so long was that lower bunks with an electrical outlet for my CPAP and sterilizer were few and sought after. I had to have a lower bunk because I was over 60 years of age, along with access to an electrical outlet. I was 68 when I went in and 70 when I came out.

Typical Three-Man Cell

As I mentioned, some inmates in Beaumont Low would be better served in a mental institution for the criminally insane. The other end of the spectrum were inmates who would be better served in an assisted living facility. This type of facility exists in the federal prison system because one in eleven (9.1%) inmates in the federal prison population is serving a life sentence with no chance for parole. For example, the federal medical facility in Springfield, Missouri is one such institution.[17] You could see the wheelchair bound inmates being wheeled by others to and from the chow hall and to other venues such as Medical, Library, or Commissary. Inmates in wheelchairs in all of the barracks were allowed to be first in line out the door of each barracks in a group move to chow, for example. For a couple of weeks, until he moved on,

---

[17] US Federal Medical Center — 1600 West Sunshine Street — Springfield, MO 65807

there was an inmate who came into Beaumont Low with a motorized wheelchair. Other wheelchair bound inmates quickly realized the potential. It surprised me the day I saw five wheelchair bound inmates "hitching a ride" with the guy in the motorized wheelchair. The motorized wheelchair was the engine and a wheelchair bound inmate had leaned forward and was holding on to the back of the chairback of the motorized wheelchair and there were four others behind him holding on to the back of the wheelchair in front of him. Inmates would step aside and laugh and applaud as they went sailing by. That spectacle ended when the motorized wheelchair bound inmate was transferred to another facility.

An inmate I became acquainted with was Marcus. Marcus was 65, which is five years younger than me. However, Marcus looked like he was in his 80's or older. His short-term memory was clearly in the senile range. Marcus told me he had been a literature professor at the University of San Diego.[18] Marcus wanted to teach in the GED program. I told him to go with me at the next Education Work Call and I would introduce him to the program director. Between when Marcus introduced himself to me in the barracks and when Education Work Call occurred at 7:30 AM the next day, Marcus tried to have the same conversation with me about every other hour. In became obvious to me during our second conversation about how he had been a literature professor at the University of San Diego, and he wanted to get a job in the GED program that Marcus had no business trying to get a job anywhere at Beaumont Low. However, not wanting to be the

---

[18] University of San Diego — 5998 Alcalá Park — San Diego, CA 92110

one to tell him that, I let him tag along with me at the next Education Work Call.

Needless to say, Marcus was not asked to stay and teach. I saw Marcus that evening in the barracks. Marcus came up to me all excited because the program director had told him he would put him on the waiting list to be a teacher in the GED program. Since I knew there was a shortage of teachers and no waiting list, obviously, the program director did not want to be the barer of bad news to Marcus any more than I did.

A few days later, an inmate that I did not know came to my cell door about 11:00 PM. I had been asleep since about 9:30 PM so when I got awake enough to actually hear what he was saying, I immediately put my pants, socks and shoes on and followed him back to his cell. It seemed that Marcus had gotten up and gone to the bathroom and then forgot where his cell was and went into this guy's cell and sat on his empty bunk. In prison, you do not sit in someone else's bunk unless you are wanting to fight them. The guy was smart enough to not just jump him when he saw Marcus sitting in his bunk. After a few words, he realized the guy was old, infirm and truly did not know where he was. So, he went to get the barracks medic, me. I, literally, took Marcus by the hand and led him back to his bunk. Marcus' two cellmates were asleep and were oblivious to Marcus' behavior or what had just happened. I also suspect they would not have helped if they had known. They would consider it to be "not their problem" which is the prevalent attitude among most inmates unless it affects them directly. There was an the inmate whose cellmate lay dead in the bunk above him for a couple of days before inmates in the neighboring cell began to investigate the stench emanating from their neighboring cell. Inmates, in general, have a very narrow view of issues that affect them. Even a dead body in the bunk above them may not be viewed as something that affects them.

At the entrance to the chow hall, in addition to boxes for the commissary list by barracks, there are boxes labeled, "Message to the Chaplain," and "Message to the Warden." I wrote the note, quoted in *italics* below, and placed a copy in the Chaplain's box and the Warden's box.

"In barracks UB, there is an inmate named Marcus Weatherly. Marcus has no short-term memory. He has to be told to bathe and forgets where his cell is if he gets up at night and goes to the bathroom. Clearly, he does not have the mental capacity to care for himself which is the standard the Beaumont Low Prison Handbook says, 'All inmates at Beaumont Low' meet this standard. The other night Marcus was found sitting in someone else's bunk because he thought it was his own. Luckily, for Marcus and the inmate in whose bunk Marcus was sitting, Marcus was not attacked. If Marcus comes to harm while in Beaumont Low, what is your liability? It will come to light that you were notified via this note that Marcus' mental capacity is not what the handbook standard states it must be."

The following day when I returned to the barracks after teaching/tutoring for the day, I was told the guard came to Marcus and escorted him to Medical. I found out later that Marcus had been sent to the medical facility in Springfield, Missouri which has an assisted living facility.[19]

Normal life, including love affairs of sorts, occurs in prison between inmates more than, at least I thought, would occur. An example was the first of

---

[19] Federal Medical Unit — 1900 West Sunshine Street — Springfield, MO 65807

several fights that occurred in the Education and Library section of the prison. My classroom was two doors down from the Library. The door between the Library and my classroom was the restroom. There were no women's inmate restrooms at Beaumont Low because all of the inmates were considered "men," even the men who considered themselves women, or inmates who considered themselves something in between. Men and women guards and staff members had their own restrooms that inmates were not allowed to use. There is that special feeling again. During my fascinating lecture on the Quadratic Formula and how to factor Quadratic Equations, there was a large thud that rattled the pictures on the back wall of my classroom. Yelling and cursing could also be heard through the wall. The other side of the wall was the inmates' restroom. You could hear the sounds of a struggle and the wall continued to shake. In the hallway, guard and staff members came running. The guards had canisters of pepper spray at the ready; all of them were heading for the restroom next door to my classroom.

When a man (or woman I suppose) is hit in the face with pepper spray, they emit a high pitch squeal, much like a pig that is calling for its mother. High pitched squeals emanated from the restroom after the first two guards entered. When guards stop a fight, they always do so two at a time. I saw a guard watching two inmates go at it and wondered why he was just watching them instead of trying to stop them. I was told later by a more experienced inmate that guards are trained to not try to stop a fight by themselves because the inmates fighting have, on occasion, teamed up against a guard who had tried to stop them from fighting. Therefore, guards are trained to wait until there is at least one more guard at the ready. The two guards approach the pair of fighting inmates and each guard picks one inmate and at the same instant they each spray the combatants in the face with pepper spray. This strategy effectively gets the fighting inmates' attention and stops the fight immediately. Each inmate, pepper sprayed, is on the floor, squealing with his hands over his eyes. This fight ended as intended with both inmates rolling on the floor of the restroom, squealing and putting their hands over their eyes. Both inmates were handcuffed with plastic handcuffs and led away to the SHU. If the guards are nice, they will stop at the Medical Department so the inmates can have their eyes irrigated with saline; almost all guards are not nice in these circumstances.

Why was there a fight you ask? An inmate/librarian who knew both combatants told me the next day when I asked him. He said,

"Howard and Ronald have been lovers for about three years and Howard is scheduled to go the camp in two weeks and wanted to end their relationship. Ronald did not want the relationship to end so he jumped Howard in the restroom so they both would end up the SHU and if Ronald has his way, Howard will be denied, at least for a while, the privilege of going to the camp." Love springs eternal...

About three months later another fight occurred. This time in the Library when two inmates who both loved another inmate decided that fighting would determine who got to "date" one of the transvestite inmates who went by the name, "Emory." Emory, I knew, because she lived in UB barracks, and she was one of the two inmates who lived in the SO section of UB barracks who asked me to treat her scalp and face when she had been attacked on her way to the restroom. Emory had winked at a Shining Path member who took offense at her flirting with him. *What's a girl to do?*

There were fights everyday somewhere in Beaumont Low. I witnessed and/or treated one or more of the combatants about two times a week. I could list the details of each fight that I witnessed and/or when I treated the combatants. While I treated the combatants, to pass the time I always asked, "Why." They were always only too happy to tell me. The top twelve reasons why inmates would (or will) come to blows are listed below. There are more reasons, but if you do not get the idea with these twelve reasons, you will not get the idea if more reasons are listed.

1. Argument over which TV program to watch.
2. Argument over who could smuggle the most food out of the chow hall without getting caught. This fight occurred between inmates who were also cellmates.
3. Argument over a push that occurred during a game of basketball in the rec yard.
4. Argument over money, how much owed, or failure to pay the debt in a timely manner.
5. Argument over who ate the last cookie in the box.
6. Argument between two inmates who both loved another.
7. Argument between three inmates who all loved another.
8. Fight because one inmate flirted with another inmate who took offense.
9. Fight between inmates for no specific reason; they just did not like one another.
10. Fight when an inmate plays his radio too loud.
11. Fight between groups of inmates within a gang when some members wanted to move up within the same gang pecking order, just like a pack of wolves.
12. Fight between groups of inmates from different gangs when members of one gang wanted to

move up in the gang pecking order between gangs, just like packs of wolves.

After any fight that the guards became aware of there is a "shakedown" of the barracks. Everyone has to go to the rec yard, and you are searched when you leave the barracks, very thoroughly. Very thoroughly through your clothes in every crevice, including your private parts, by whatever male or female guard is ready when you leave the barracks. There are five or six guards ready to search inmates when they leave the barracks. In groups of five or six, inmates all walk out of the barracks at the same time and are directed to stand spread eagled in front of a guard while each of them is searched. Most cells are trashed during the shakedown. Trashed means everything from bedding to toilet articles would be in a big pile in the middle of your cell upon your return. The only thing they never messed with for me was my CPAP unit and SoClean sterilizer. These would be sitting in my empty bunk. The guards had to have carefully lifted them up, jerked the mattress and bedding out from underneath and set them back down. I always appreciated that.

Shakedowns occurred after fights because guards wanted to find shivs and other weapons, as well as drugs, alcohol, tobacco, K2 (synthetic marijuana), cell phones, and pornography. These items are all common contraband, along with the Charles Stinger. They never found the Charles Stingers and I asked Sam where they were hidden because they found all of the other contraband items. Sam smiled and said,

"They are hidden in the one place we know that no one, even inmates as well as guards, will never touch. They're hidden behind the religious book section in the barracks Library."

I responded,

"That's a stroke of genius; praise be to God!"

There is a separation between Hispanic inmates. It is between those who were raised in the United States and identify with white inmates more than Hispanic inmates who are from Mexico, Puerto Rico, Central or South America. Ricardo and José were raised in the United States, so they are included with Sam's White Guys. José was moving into the lower bunk in the cell next door and giving up the lower bunk that had an electrical outlet next to it. José had to have a lower bunk because he was over 60, but he did not need an electrical outlet. The bunk José was moving to was going to be vacated when Jesus, the guy who made cheesecake from coffee creamer and the graham crackers and vanilla wafers I provided, went home in a few weeks. It took me about three months to cultivate the friendship with both Harold, Ricardo and José. Then another three months for a vacancy somewhere that José was willing to move to. In the meantime, I started another adventure.

Chapter VI
Running with The Shining Path

Manuel was one of my cellmates in the ten-man cell (chicken coop). Manuel had been a high school physical education teacher just outside Mexico City. Manuel found he could make a lot more money in Mexico driving a truck in his broken English, "on the long road." On the long road, meant from the border of Mexico with Guatemala and Belize across Mexico and into the United States. Manuel made good money driving the truck, but he paid too little attention to what his cargo was. When a US-ICE[20] roadblock stopped his truck in New Mexico about fifty miles north of the Mexican border, a search of his trailer revealed fifteen illegal immigrants in the back of his truck. Manuel was sentenced to five years in a Federal Prison followed by deportation back to Mexico. Manuel was within sixty days of the completion of his sentence. Manuel was also the barracks tailor and medic. If you needed pants hemmed or a belt loop re-attached professionally, Manuel was the guy. Being the medic, Manual had a large first aid kit that he could replenish as needed by visiting the Medical Dispensary at any sick call which occurred daily at 6:30 AM and 12:30 PM.

Since Manuel was leaving, the barracks needed another medic and tailor. The guy who ironed my shirts, also named José, volunteered to be the tailor and Manuel and my other cellmates asked me to volunteer to be the medic. I am not sure why they asked me. Perhaps it was because Manuel was in the bunk next to me in the chicken coop, or because they knew from me just talking about my

---

[20] US-ICE – United States Immigration and Customs Enforcement

background that I had taught first aid and had once been certified in both CPR and AED operation. The high value placed on the barracks medic job I did not initially realize. So, I got Manuel's first aid kit to put under my bunk and refresher courses in CPR and AED.[21] Both courses took four hours on a Tuesday afternoon in the Medical Department. At the time, Manuel's most important routine duty, as the barracks medic, involved dressing Senõr González's sore on his right stump about three inches above his knee. Senõr González's right leg below the knee had been amputated about five years earlier due to complications from diabetes. The sore on his leg was continually aggravated by the prothesis (artificial leg) he wore almost all the time. Senõr González, is the head of The Shining Path cartel for all of Beaumont (Low, Medium, Max and Camp) and probably lots of other places I came to suspect. Senõr González is the spitting image of Henry Kissinger and the voice to match except in Spanish. Senõr González, I learned, was from Peru but was living in Mexico City when he was arrested and extradited to the United States. He is serving a life sentence with no parole because he was a leader of The Shining Path cartel.

Senõr González, being at the top of the inmate hierarchy, resided in the only two man cell in the barracks. His cell mate was Gary Buena. Gary was Mexican American and had a law degree from the University of New Mexico. Gary handled correspondence for Senõr González and also acted as translator for him. Senõr González never spoke English to anyone who was not in his intimate circle who did not speak Spanish. Even the guards were deferential to him.

---

[21] CPR – Cardiopulmonary Resuscitation | AED – Automatic Cardio Defibrillator

Manuel changed the dressing on Senõr González's sore every other day and rubbed Cortisone ointment on it and redressed it. Manuel brought me to the cell, introduced me to Senõr González and Gary Buena and told them I was going to be the new barracks medic upon his departure in about five weeks at that point. I treated Senõr González's sore as Manuel had taught me while Manuel watched. Senõr González did not say anything, but I could sense he was paying close attention to me as was Gary. Senõr González's two bodyguards, Ortega and Bonito, who occupied cells on either side of Senõr González's cell – one bodyguard in each adjacent cell were also standing over me paying close attention.

Ortega and Bonito could be twins – six feet five inches plus and each weighing in excess of three hundred pounds. Ortega and Bonito spoke surprisingly good English. They were also the barracks enforcers. If an inmate ignored inmates' rules or was bullying anyone, the enforcers would visit them either when they were sleeping or in the shower, e.g., when they were most vulnerable. Anyone who had experienced a visit – either night or shower – looked like they had done fifteen rounds with Muhamad Ali in his prime and their ribs would be badly bruised or broken. The first visit was the mildest visit. If they did not get the message from the first visit, they were visited again. The second visit always resulted in them being carried out on a stretcher in need of life support or beyond life support. In inmate jargon, if an inmate was beyond life support, "they had been sent to a better place."

I came to learn firsthand about night visits because, as the barracks medic, I got to patch up an inmate after he had incurred a night visit. To prevent a second visit, he told the guards he had slipped in the shower and no one was at fault, but himself. I put seventeen stitches in his nose and forehead. Of course, the guards did not believe him, but could not or would not pursue it. This particular inmate, I do not recall his name, had made a snide remark and pushed one of the prettier transsexuals in the barracks. And, either she or one of her followers, complained to Senõr González. Senõr González did not tolerate bullying. He did not tolerate bullying because of any interest in whoever was being bullied, but because if the guards became aware of anyone being bullied, the whole barracks would be put under lockdown until the bully was identified and removed. Lockdown means, no email, no telephone, no commissary, no rec yard and no TV for anyone. Inmate justice, under the cartel, is swift, certain and severe with no chance for appeal. Men who flaunted the rules of society all their lives, after a night visit, or faced with the threat of a night visit, or shower visit, became diligent followers of inmate rules in the barracks.

One of many epiphanies I had in prison was the fact that at Beaumont Low there were murderers, bank robbers, pedophiles and all sorts of men who had done violent, evil things along with white collar criminals. I suppose I am considered a white-collar criminal, at least my fellow inmates put me in this category. The reason these violent criminals are in the low security prison is they have earned the right to be there. They had started out five or ten years earlier in the maximum-security prison. If they had obeyed the rules for three years or more, without incident, they got moved to the medium security prison, after the same process occurred in the medium security prison, they were moved to the low security prison. However, their potential for violence remained with them, and if they screwed up, they started back at the maximum-security prison and had to perform all over again to get back to the low.

There are actually more violent confrontations in the low security prison then in the medium or maximum-security prisons – hence Bloody Beaumont refers to the low security prison even by the inmates themselves. Why is that the case you ask? It is because in the maximum-security prison, inmates are in two-man cells and their food is brought to them. Prior to moving outside their cell, they "shackle up." That means they stand with their back against the barred door of the cell with their hands and feet next to the bars. A guard reaches through the bars and places shackles around their ankles and handcuffs on their wrists. Then, and only then, are they allowed out of their cell. The only person they have contact with when not in shackles and handcuffs is their cellmate or "celli" in prison jargon. And, since their celli is also in the maximum-security unit, it is certain they also are either prone to violence or capable of it. If you attack your celli in the maximum-security unit, it will be a fight to the death. Therefore, fights in the maximum-security unit are rare, if nonexistent, because inmates do not get the chance to be violent with anyone except their celli and the stakes are too high in that confrontation.

The medium security prison, I was told by those who had been there, is just like the low security prison except there are barred doors on the cells and inmates are locked in at 10:00 PM until 6:00 AM every day of the week. Between the hours of 6:00 AM and 10:00 PM you can go to your job when the work call occurs and go to their chow hall , their education, their rec yard, their Library, and their commissary at the appropriate times. I was also told the food at the chow hall in the medium was much better than the food at the low. That is easy to believe because the bar at the low chow hall was set so incredibly low. In fact, inmates told me, "low" also refers to the quality of the food, not just the level of security at Beaumont Low.

I now had two jobs at Beaumont Low – teacher/tutor in the GED program and barracks medic. Senõr González's sore on his leg looked bad. It was three inches in length, about a quarter inch wide and a half inch deep at its deepest point. All the layers of skin were gone, you could see what looked like muscle tissue, and it was dry. It did not drain and Senõr González said there was no pain when I filled it with Cortisone. After two weeks of dressing this sore every other day, it was apparent to me that it was not getting better, and it seemed to be getting bigger.

Luckily, one of my sisters is a retired registered nurse. I got her on the visitors' list and sent her an email that described Senõr González's sore, its cause and what I did to treat it along with the frequency of treatment. My sister gave me excellent advice. She said,

"Stop the Cortisone and start using a Triple Antibiotic Ointment. Also, start massaging his leg from the groin to the sore while using a circulation enhancer such as Deep Heat. Start doing this daily until you see improvement in circulation and/or the sore begins to get smaller. Then go to every other day but continue the same treatment."

The very next day, which was an off day for treating Senõr González's sore, I went to Medical and explained to the nurse what my sister, also a nurse, had said to do. The Medical Department nurse responded,

"She is right; I should have thought of that."

She gave me six tubes of triple antibiotic ointment and six rolls of gauze and medical tape.

The next day at 3:45 PM when I got back from my teaching/tutoring job I got the first aid kit, tape, gauze, and antibiotic ointment and headed to Senõr González's cell. Gary was not there, so I woke up Bonito in the next cell who was napping and told him my treatment plan and that Gary was not there. Bonito got up and went in to Senõr González's cell with me and explained in Spanish what I had in mind for Senõr González. Senõr González nodded his okay and I started. After 20 minutes of massage, I filled the sore with the antibiotic ointment and redressed it. I told Bonito I needed to do it every day until it began to get better, then I would go back to every other day. Halfway through the translation to him, Senõr González held up his hand for Bonito to be quiet, Senõr González looked at me, leaned forward and kissed me on the forehead and in perfect English said,

"You're an okay guy, let's move you closer to me."

In the next week, Jesus, the cake guy, left for home and José moved into Jesus' bunk in the cell next door to his. The next day I had just got back to my cell from teaching/tutoring and Senõr González's bodyguards/enforcers, Ortega and Bonito, came into my cell and Ortega said to me,

"We've come for you."

For a split second, I was terrified, but then Bonito added,
"Is this your locker."

I said,

"Yes."

With that, Bonito picked up my locker, contents and all, and walked out. Bonito disconnected my CPAP unit and sterilizer and put them in the middle of my bunk, he put my boots and first aid kit in the middle of my mattress and then rolled everything up, including three blankets, picked it all up and walked out. I followed meekly behind and my cellmates silently waved goodbye as I walked out. In about three minutes I was in my new cell. It was directly across from the communal showers, toilets, sinks and urinals and in the middle of The Shining Path section of UB barracks. They even made up my bunk, hooked up my CPAP unit and sterilizer, and put my extra boots and first aid kit under the bunk. All I had to do was walk from the ten-man cell – cell number 61 – to cell number 54. I was two cells down from Senõr González's cell.

My cellmates, Ricardo and Harold, I subsequently learned, were also a part of The Shining Path in that they had been dealers or distributors of cocaine for The Shining Path on the outside. Ricardo had been in Kansas City and Harold had been in Memphis. I did not fully realize the magnitude of what had happened to me with the move, but it began to be apparent immediately. A few minutes after I moved to my new cell, I decided to take a shower and got my shower stuff together, walked across the aisle and stood at the back of the line. There were six men in front of me. I had not paid attention to the talk among the six because it was in Spanish, but when the guy in the shower got finished and walked out the six guys in front of me turned to me and motioned for me to go to the front of the line and take the shower. I said,

"I can wait."

The guy immediately in front of me said,

"You can't do that sir, if Senõr González, hears that someone disrespected you they will get a night visit; don't set them up for that."

I went to the front of the line. I no longer had to wait to shave or brush my teeth either. This perk continued until I left and went to the halfway house ten months later.

Senõr González's sore began to heal slowly and after six weeks of daily dressings and massages, it was half the size it had been. I changed the protocol to every other day until the only evidence left was a small indentation about two inches long where it had been.

I continued in the roll of barracks medic until sixty days prior to my release. José, the guy who did my ironing and who was also the barracks tailor when Manuel left, had a cellmate, named Rafael. Rafael had been a medic in the Mexican Army prior to joining the Sureños which is a rival gang to The Shining Path cartel. However, the Sureños were almost gone. Rafael and about four others were the only members of the Sureños in UB barracks. All of them had come into the barracks after the many members of the Sureños had been shipped out due to their leadership and participation in the UB barracks riot. José, whom I had told that I as about two months away from leaving, told me Rafael would be a good candidate for the barracks medic job. José also told me that Rafael was a member of the Sureños, but Rafael said he would be the barracks medic for everyone. I thought about it for a day and asked Harold and Sam if they knew of anyone, they would want for the barracks medic job. I also told them Rafael, as a medic in the Mexican army, was more qualified than I was to be the barracks medic, but he was member of the Sureños. Sam said,

"I'll have a talk with Rafael and let you know."

The next day Sam said,

"I've had the talk with Rafael, and I think he's okay for the barracks medic job but go ask Senõr González."

I asked Senõr González later that evening and Senõr González said,

"Go get Rafael, I want to talk to him."

I brought Rafael to Senõr González's cell and waited with Ortega and Bonito in the next cell where they were playing chess. In about ten minutes, Senõr González called to me. I went into the cell and Senõr González said,

"Start training Rafael to be the next barracks medic."

I had successfully found my replacement for the barracks medic job.

After I turned over the barracks medic job to Rafael, I did not see Senõr González very often. Gary, Senõr González's celli came to me one day in the Library and said,

"Senõr González has stopped taking insulin, and he's not eating anything much. I think he's had enough of this."

I said,

"I don't know how to help him, or what to say to him or you or anyone about it."

Gary said,

"Neither do I."

I stopped by Senõr González's cell that afternoon, but he was asleep. He drifted into and

out of sleep for about two weeks and then one Saturday morning as I was getting ready for my wife's visit, I saw medics coming down the hallway with a stretcher. I knew which cell they were going to before they got there. They stopped in front of Senõr González's cell and went in. After a couple of minutes, they had him strapped in the stretcher and walked back past my cell. Senõr González just looked like he was asleep. One of the medics said to me,
"He's in a diabatic coma. I don't think he's going to make it."

All I ever found out about Senõr González's fate was from a medical orderly who lived in barracks UB. He told me that they had transferred Senõr González to a federal medical facility somewhere. I suspect Senõr González died, but I do not know his whereabouts or his fate.

After Senõr González left, there was a leadership vacuum in The Shining Path, but no one stepped up to take charge. Bonito, Ortega and Gary would answer questions. The questions usually involved what to do about an inmate who was behind on his debt payments. Sometimes they even asked me what I thought should be done and when asked, I always said to get them on a payment plan because putting them in medical or the SHU did not get anyone paid back, but a payment plan would get at least some of what was owed paid back.

I had also told the GED program director I was leaving in sixty days and he said he and I should begin to look for a replacement for me. I was never around anyone who was remotely qualified to teach in the GED program, so I did not ask anyone. However, thirty days before I left, a mechanical engineer had landed in Beaumont Low for a thirty-six-month sentence, named Gavin. I never asked and therefore, never found out, why he was there, but Gavin started to sit in on my classes and tutoring sessions. After three days, Gavin said he was ready to take my place so for two days I sat down and let Gavin teach and tutor and he did well. I told the GED program director that Gavin was a good teacher and tutor. He responded,

"Then I wish you well and you can go your way."

The last day, I stood up in each class and bid them goodbye and for the last three weeks, I did not have a job. I went to the Library every day at the 7:30 AM work call and read to pass the time.

Chapter VII
The Role of Counselor and Confessor

Rise from newbe to a member of a cartel's inner circle...

Initially, I was a "newbe." I was someone, not gang affiliated, not a repeat offender and my charge was not in the SO category. In addition, I was not a former policeman, prison guard, or prosecuting attorney. Because I am over 60 years of age, I was accorded some degree of respect. My status grew pretty rapidly from newbe to trusted member of The Shining Path's inner circle. This happened through no conscious effort on my part. All I did was get a job as a Teacher/Tutor in the GED program because I was bored sitting in the barracks all day. This job allowed me to hang out in the Library which is two doors from my classroom.

I believe the rise from newbe to a cartel's inner circle started when I met Gary Buena, Senõr González's cellmate, in the Library. Gary hung out there during the day and prepared appeals and pleas for inmates who wanted to rid themselves of pending charges while serving their federal sentence. Gary charged $20 commissary, or 18 stamps for the filing. Gary was overwhelmed with the filings. I, by chance, sat down next to him during a break in the afternoon's tutoring session because no one had shown up that needed tutoring. Gary knew I was a teacher/tutor in the GED program, and he asked me what my educational background was. I told him I had BS and MS Degrees in chemical engineering as well as an MBA. Gary thought for a minute and said,

"Do you want to do court filings?"

I said,

"I've done filings for EPA and state equivalent agency related activities surrounding operational and environmental permitting. That means I can write in complete sentences and they are grammatically correct. What do the court filings involve?"

Gary showed me two filings he had just completed. The trick was knowing where to get the forms from the internet on the computer in the Legal Department. Inmates do not have access to the internet except from illicit iPhones. The Legal Department's computer could access the internet, but it had been programmed to only access websites with the notation, "...gov" at the end of the website. This allowed access to any state, county or city court that had a website in the United States. When you accessed a court for a form, I was instructed to print out six duplicates and put the ones you do not use into a file for that particular court. This action built a database of commonly used forms and saved time. When you used the last form for a particular court, you were supposed to access that court's website and print out six more forms. The entire filing was usually three or four handwritten pages along with the court form. The court form required the inmate's signature. The handwritten pages consisted of...

✓ Cover Letter – introduced the inmate, stated where he was incarcerated, and it also provided...

- A description of the federal charge for which he was serving time.
- The case number of the federal charge.
- The initial date of his incarceration.
- The final or "out date" of his incarceration assuming good time days are not taken away in the interim.

- The docket number of the pending charge of the court he was writing to (the court he was filing his plea to).
- This statement, *"I wish to plead guilty to this case, docket number XXX, and serve my time concurrently with the federal sentence for which I am currently serving time."*
- The inmate's address that was making the filing and the statement, *"Please write 'LEGAL MAIL' on the envelope next to my address."* This statement was to prevent legal mail inmates received from being opened by censors. All inmates' non-legal mail is censored. Inmates' outgoing mail is not censored.

✓ The form from the court to which the inmate is making his plea.

- *This form included the docket number of the pending case.*
- *A space for the inmate to dispute or agree to the pending charges.*
- *A duplicate of the "I wish to plead guilty..." statement in the cover letter.*
- *A space for the inmate's signature.*
- *Some of the court forms also included a space for a witness to the inmate's signature. In these instances, I put my name and signature as the witness.*

Pleading guilty did add to their rap sheet but serving time in a federal prison for dealing in cocaine or transporting illegal aliens pretty well ended their hopes and dreams of a vanilla life upon their release, regardless of what else was on their rap sheet. I started doing about four filings a week and it tapered off to two or three a month after three months. Also,

I did not charge anything for producing the filing because I had all the commissary money I could spend and had no addictions, such as K2. Most inmates do not realize the value of inmates' "good will" in a prison.

An unanticipated consequence of these free court filings were requests from inmates to assist them in writing letters to loved ones, and for general advice on relationships with women or family members, including parental advice. I searched in the Library and found there is actually a book entitled, Remote Parenting. Remote Parenting is how to parent from a distance due to being in the military or other job-related position that requires extended periods away from family members as well as divorce and incarceration. I read the book and provided advice to inmates from it. Just telling inmates to "read the book" would not suffice since most inmates are not used to reading anything. And, at Beaumont Low, most inmates are Hispanic and most speak English, but a substantial number could not read English, let alone write English. Several times I wrote out what an inmate needed to say to a loved one, and another inmate would translate it into Spanish for the inmate since usually the person he was writing to did not understand written English well enough to grasp the meaning in the letter. So, court petition filer, letter writer and counselor became my third job.

Prior to being a court filer, letter writer and counselor, I already was a GED Teacher/Tutor and UB Barracks Medic. At this point, I was considered a trusted member of the Shining Path and one of the few that was not Hispanic and the only member, other than Gary, that did not have any tattoos whatsoever.

A couple of weeks after I moved to cell number 54, I began to have inmates who were not a part of The Shining Path come to me for advice. It was advice, mostly on what to say in an email or letter to a girl friend or wife, but sometimes it was a letter to an attorney or court. One inmate came to me, clearly terribly upset, because of a letter he had received from his wife. They corresponded regularly, and he said,

"Right out of the clear blue I get this letter and in it she says she has been diagnosed with Psoriasis!"

I said,

"Okay, so why are you so upset?"

He says,

"Because I've been in here for five years, why the Hell do you think I'm upset?"

It only then occurred to me that he thought Psoriasis was an STD (Sexually Transmitted Disease)! I said,

"Psoriasis is not an STD; it is skin a disease that is caused by an overactive immune system and is usually aggravated by stress. Your wife is probably stressed because you are in here and it has nothing to do with having sex with anyone."

He was greatly relieved. I helped him write a letter to his wife that was kind and understanding and for the first time in any letter, according to him, he asked about her problems and how she was coping with him being gone. After that letter, I had almost daily, an inmate waiting for me when I returned from teaching/tutoring with a letter writing request.

It was on a Thursday at lunch that I met Denis Stremlakoff. Denis sat down at my table and introduced himself. He said he had heard about my court filings and he had checked me out by asking

Senõr González about me. Denis was in barracks VA, where Raoul was housed. Denis was from Russia and had a successful "Labor and Immigration Service" business. On the outside the business is called "Human Trafficking." Denis was serving a life sentence without parole and was sort of a lesser equivalent in VA barracks to what Senõr González was in UB barracks.

There were a number of Russian mafia members at Beaumont spread among the maximum, medium and low prisons and they all pledged their allegiance to Denis as far as I could tell. Denis wanted to know if I played chess and told me that he had trouble finding someone who could give him a challenge. I said I used to play in college and was very rusty, but I would give it a try. We met in the rec yard at a picnic table the next afternoon and played two games. Denis won both, but the second game I almost won except I got overconfident at the end. From that time on, we met three times per week – Tuesday, Thursday and Sunday in the afternoon in the rec yard or the building next to the rec yard where there are pool tables and tables for cards, chess and other board games. After losing six games, I started winning about half of them which pleased Denis. Denis would reminisce about Ufa, the city in the Russian Urals where he is from. He missed it terribly along with his wife and two daughters whom he will never see in person, but he gets pictures of them from his former wife whom he still loves. His former wife, with his blessing, divorced him and married his brother so she and his daughters could have a better life than if she tried to raise their daughters by herself or worse, met and married someone outside the family.

Every inmate has a sad story to tell, and some stories are sadder than others. I met an inmate while walking to the medical department to get more supplies for my first aid kit and he started a conversation with me. He asked how long I was in and I told him sadly,

"I'm here for about fifteen more months in a twenty-four-month sentence, and my wife is having a worse time of it than me."

He said,

"You're lucky you have someone on the outside, I'm in here for thirty-five more years. I got in here by myself and I'll leave by myself."

The recidivism[22] in federal prisons is about 40% for nonviolent crimes and 64% for violent crimes. In fact, most of the inmates I grew close to considered being in prison "normal," and outside an odd or even frightening existence. In prison jargon, ending your sentence and going to the outside is called, "going around the bend until you're back again."

I developed a reputation for having good taste in murder mystery novels. Since I worked next door to the Library, I took whatever novel I wanted without checking it out (the inmate/librarians did not care) and when finished I would either take it back to the Library or put it in the barracks Library which was a room across the hall from the White Guys TV room. The contents of this Library were changed monthly with the main Library, except for the religious book section which never changed and which I never saw used. Inmates would occasionally come to my cell after dinner and ask for my recommendation of what murder mystery novel they might enjoy. I introduced probably a dozen inmates to the wonders of Agatha Christi murder mysteries, and Sir Arthur Conan Doyle's Sherlock Holmes.

---

[22] recidivism – the tendency of a criminal to commit the same type of offense upon release and serving time again for the same crime

Often, while discussing what they would enjoy reading, they would also confess their hopes, dreams and aspirations. I do not know why. I found their hopes, dreams and aspirations not fanciful, but practical and even doable upon their release if they did not succumb to the habits that got them into prison.

For example, two guys who both work in the chow hall, and one has graduated from the prison culinary arts school are planning to open a Tex-Mex restaurant in Amarillo, Texas where one of them is from upon their release. They get out within six months of each other. I have never been to Amarillo, but I do know that in Texas there can never be enough Tex-Mex restaurants. I do not know where the money will come from, but they both talked about their girlfriends on the outside who share their dream and have begun to communicate with each other. There is another inmate whose wife is in prison on the same set of charges that he is serving. However, she is in the federal prison in Chowchilla, California.[23] They are each planning on going to truck driving school, an eight week course, upon their release and his wife is going to try to get a long haul trucking job prior to his release since she gets out eighteen months before his release. Upon his release, after his eight-week truck driving course, they will become a long-haul truck driving team. They have spent almost ten years, from 25 to 35 years of age, in prison. They intend to see the country and be on the move always to make up for the portion of their lives they lost to prison. They have not seen each other for over ten years so far, but they talk and write to each other daily.

---

[23] CCWF — Central California Women's Facility — 23370 Road 22, Chowchilla, CA 93610

Frank, an inmate I did not know well, but I had seen him in the TV room and at Thursday's lunch. Frank came to my cell just before dinner chow call and asked to see me in the barracks Library after dinner. I told him that I would be in my cell when he got back from dinner and if came and got me, we would go to the Library and talk. He thanked me and left. After dinner, Frank came and got me, and we walked down the hall to the Library. There were no other inmates in the Library. Frank was a big man and had been an enforcer at Beaumont Low until Ortega and Bonito arrived, so he was respected. As soon as we sat down, Frank looked at me with tears in his eyes and could not speak for crying. I asked him if I could get him a cup of coffee and he said,

"Yes, please."

The only coffee I had was decaf, so I made two cups and brought them back to the Library. I did not tell Frank it was decaf coffee; that did not seem important. By the time I got back, Frank was in control of himself and started to talk. As best as I can remember, Frank said,

"My daughter is coming to visit me tomorrow. She is 23 years old now and the last time I saw her was here in prison when she was 15. She is engaged to be married and her fiancé is bringing her. My ex-wife did not want her to have a relationship with me after I went to prison, and I only saw her when she was 15 because she told her mother that was what she wanted for her birthday. When she visited then, her mother stayed in the car in the parking lot and didn't come in to see me. I don't know what to do tomorrow. Do you have any advice?"

I asked Frank how long he had been in prison, and how much longer did he have to go, Frank said,

"I'm 17 years into a 35-year sentence so I'm about halfway through. She'll be over 40 and I'll be in my 70's when I get out."

Thinking fast, I said the only things I could think of off the top of my head. I tried to put myself in the position of being a father who has been in prison for my daughter's entire lifetime beyond infancy. What do you say to her now at 23 years of age when she is about to be married? I said,

"Tell her this...'You have grown into a beautiful, kind and thoughtful young lady. I know you are kind and thoughtful, because you've come to visit your father who's been in prison your entire life beyond infancy. I know you are beautiful because I can see you. In fact, you are beautiful inside and outside.

Turn to her fiancé and say, you are a lucky young man. If you treat her as you should, she will remain beautiful and kind to you no matter how old you both are and no matter what happens to you both. My life can only serve to provide to you an example of how not to live. I loved your mother, but I thought giving her things was what I should do to make her happy. Selling drugs was the way to make the most money I could, and I knew at the time I wouldn't get caught. I was about your age when I did get caught and I've been in prison ever sense.

I've lived with the knowledge that our daughter was raised by a single mom and with not very much money. I have lived with the knowledge that I was the one that brought my daughter and her mother to that kind of life. After a few years, I even hoped her mother would find someone, but if she ever dated anyone, I never knew it. Along the way, her mother has become bitter toward me, and I don't blame her. She deserved better than she got with me. I will tell you this, 'Listen to your bride and do what she wants you do to. The voice in your head that says, if I take this job, I'll make more money and we'll be happier, is what I listened to and did, and that was wrong. Talk to each other a lot and make decisions based on long-term results together. I can't be physically with you as you grow older, but I want to hear from you. If you'll write to me, I'll write to you.'"

I finished with,

"If you say this to them, it will set the stage for what they are going to say to you and perhaps cause them to want to continue to see you."

Frank sat very still for a couple of minutes and then said,

"Do you have any notebook paper? I want to write down what you said, and I don't think I can remember it and say it unless I write it down now and read it over before their visit."

I gave him my spare legal pad and a new ball point pen and sat there while he wrote. Occasionally, he would ask me to repeat part of it. After about an hour he was satisfied and tore the page off the legal pad and gave the pad back to me, and asked,

"Can I keep the pen for a while in case I think of something else?"

I told him to keep the pen as long as he wanted and left him sitting alone in the Library. Never, in my wildest dreams, did I think life in Beaumont Low would involve this kind of encounter.

Some version of this kind of encounter occurred to me a couple of times a month during my stay there. Except for the severely deranged inmates, there is a sad story, not only for the inmate, but for those left to pick up the pieces when they go away to prison for months, years, decades or life. Police shows on TV are for entertainment, and they usually end with capture or the verdict, but in real life, there is another story that starts after the capture and verdict, and for the people involved, it is always the saddest story there is to tell.

Before the southeast Texas summer fully arrived, I took advantage of going to the rec yard about twice a week when I had backup for the tutoring session, or no one showed up for tutoring. The rec yard was open to everyone before the COVID-19 Pandemic precautions from 12:30 PM until 3:45 PM. Saturday and Sunday afternoons, when I did not have visitation, was especially attractive. I played chess with Denis outside at a picnic table. Occasionally I would walk either the short or long circuits that surrounded the rec yard. The short circuit was a cinder ash track about one fourth mile in length, and the long circuit was a cinder block path one half mile in length.

The first time I went to the rec yard was a "you can't make this stuff up moment." There before me were perhaps 150 inmates. Some lifting weights outside by the weightlifting building, some playing basketball or handball. At one end were eight inmates kneeling on mats, praying and bowing toward Mecca. To top it all off, were several, really in shape African American inmates running wind sprints and then high stepping to a familiar tune I could not remember until I had watched them several times and heard it repeated, and then I remembered! It is the tune the Wicked Witch's Monkey Soldiers hummed while marching in The

Wizard of Oz![24] Truly, my only thought was, "You can't make this stuff up!"

Perhaps the most poignant real-life story I encountered while at Beaumont Low was Julio's. Julio was 24 years old when I met him. He had started his prison career at 18 years old at Beaumont's maximum-security prison for being part of a liquor store robbery gone bad. He was driving the getaway car and one of his partners shot and killed the liquor store owner during the robbery. Julio was sentenced to 25 years to life at 18 years of age. Prison reform, called the Second Chance Act, made him eligible for parole at 25 years of age if he had a GED, someplace to live, and a job waiting.

There are prison correspondence groups that write to prisoners who have no family on the outside, and no one to write to. Most, I believe, have religious affiliations like a Baptist or Catholic Church. Letters from inmates to those outside are not censored. Letters to inmates from the outside, except legal mail, are censored. Therefore, sexy pictures and correspondence to inmates do not make it past the censors. Julio was from New Orleans and had been corresponding with a woman from a Baptist Church in New Orleans. Julio was part Cajun (white) with an African American mother. He had dreadlocks halfway down his back and did nothing but run and lift weights. He was six feet tall and 200 pounds with muscles beyond Arnold Schwarzenegger's best year. Julio was also a GED student in my algebra class. Julio stayed after the tutoring session at 3:30 PM on a Friday and I could tell he was building up to something. The GED test was about two weeks away and I thought he was going to ask me for extra help studying for it. Julio did not live in UB barracks so getting help after normal teaching/tutoring hours

---

[24] "OOH EE OOH, EE OOH OOH"

would only be possible, without breaking rules, in the evening at the Library from 6:30 PM to 8:30 PM.

However, Julio wanted help for something else. He had been corresponding with a woman, named Jeanette, who was 27 years old from a Baptist Church prison correspondence group in New Orleans where Julio was from. The letter writing with Jeanette had been going on for three years. Julio told me she was a registered nurse and was currently working with disabled veterans at a VA Hospital in New Orleans. The thing that scared Julio was that they both knew he was eligible for parole in six months when he turned 25, if he had a place to live, and a job waiting. In Jeanette's last letter, she wanted to come to Beaumont Low and visit him in person. Julio was afraid she would not like him when she saw him. Julio confessed in a low whisper he had never been with a girl and never had a close relationship with anyone, male or female, in his life. He was an only child, raised in the sixth ward in New Orleans (bad slum) by a single mother who made a living as a hotel maid at minimum wage; he never knew his father. Julio wanted my help in responding to Jeanette's last letter requesting a visit.

I told Julio I would help him, and we set a meeting the next morning, a Saturday, in the Library at 8:30 AM. I told Julio to bring Jeanette's last three letters. Jeanette had written over the last three letters that she wanted a long-term relationship with someone, and Julio had said he did too. Jeanette also said she lived in a two-bedroom apartment and it was big enough for the two of them. In addition, she had a friend that managed the New Orleans Athletic Club in the French Quarter in New Orleans who said he had a job as a fitness instructor waiting for him upon his release. Julio was terrified he would screw it all up either in the letter, or during her visit. He wanted my advice on everything from his haircut to what to say to her during her visit. I could not be with him during his visit because his visitation number[25] was even and mine was odd.

The response to Jeanette's last letter asking for a visit was easy. As we sat in the Library, I wrote the letter for him. All he had to do was copy it in his own handwriting. I wrote as if I were him,

"Of course, I want you to visit, I have been wanting to ask you for some time but was afraid you would say 'no' and would stop writing to me. I'm a fitness nut and my dream job is to be a physical fitness instructor at a health club, spa, or assisting disabled veterans. I don't have the formal education as a fitness instructor. I'm just really fit. I'll have my GED when I get out and I'll keep going to school part-time. I would like to get a degree in physical education.

Two weeks from now is my visitation weekend. Visitation weekends are the even weekends of the month. Could you please come in two weeks?

Love,

Julio"

I also told him, as a rule, women were not attracted to men whose hair was longer than theirs so he should get his dreadlocks shortened or removed. My last piece of advice to him was to relax be himself and be especially blunt about his fears of being on the outside and the fact he had never had a close relationship with anyone in his life. In one of Jeanette's letters, she had said they could convert her guest bedroom into a workout room for both of

---

[25] visitation number — the fifth digit of an inmate's BOP ID Number. Even numbered inmates had visitation on even weekends during the month and odd numbered inmates' visitation was on odd weekends.

them. Julio said he had never even dared to dream about having a woman like Jeanette in his life. He did not know what she looked like but could tell she was black (his words) from her voice on the phone. He also knew she liked to jog for exercise, and she lived in the Garden District, which is next to the French Quarter, and that she jogged around the French Quarter during for her workouts. Two weeks from the day that I helped him with his letter was his visitation weekend. We both, Julio more than me, were extremely excited about the upcoming visit from Jeanette. The visitation Saturday came and went. All I knew was that visitation had occurred, but since it was not my weekend, I did not know until Monday in my algebra class how Julio had fared.

Julio walked into my classroom grinning from ear to ear and I knew without him saying anything that it had been a success. Julio was movie star good looking with a bodybuilder's body and funky short dreadlock hairdo with pearly white, naturally straight teeth. I am sure Julio is many women's (and some men's) dream of what a man should look like. I would have liked to have seen Jeanette's reaction when Julio walked in and she realized this was her letter writing boyfriend. Julio told me all about the visit and that Jeanette had dreadlocks halfway down her back and was almost as tall as him and in great physical condition like a marathon runner. Before Julio left Beaumont, he told me he was going to ask Jeanette to marry him. I told him to wait until they have lived together at least 30 days before popping the question. Prison is kind of like the Army in that you meet people, become close to them, and when your time together is over, you never see or hear from them again. I wonder if Julio and Jeanette are living happily ever after?

Ricardo, my former cellmate, came to my cell one evening and said,

"I'm leaving for home in the morning. My wife drove to her sister's house in Houston yesterday, and she'll be here at 7:30 in the morning to pick me up. I've been in thirteen years."

This prison stint was Ricardo's second time to serve. The first time was seven years for drug dealing. He was out four years and caught fifteen years for the same offense and served the thirteen years that finished in the morning. Good behavior, and the Second Chance Act, cut two years off his sentence. Ricardo told me if he caught a third sentence for the same offense, it was life without parole, and he said,

"I'm done now. My brother-in-law has a job waiting for me in his tire store in Kansas City."

Ricardo got married while he was in prison. He had corresponded with the girl that is now his wife for about thirteen years — his entire second stint in prison. Her name is Evelyn and she is an emergency room nurse in a major Kansas City hospital. Evelyn had been the wife of a childhood friend of Ricardo's but had divorced him several years earlier. Evelyn got Ricardo's address from Ricardo's mother and had started writing to him when he first arrived for his second stint in the federal prison system. After six years of writing almost every day to each other, Ricardo asked her to marry him, and she said, "Yes." Evelyn drove to Forest City; the federal prison Ricardo was in at the time.[26] They were married in the prison chapel by the chaplain. If any couple qualifies for a happy marriage, and a long and prosperous life, they qualify!

---

[26] Forrest City Correctional Institution — 1400 Dale Bumpers Road — Forrest City, AR 72335

Ricardo had been transferred from Forrest City to Beaumont because he had been caught flying a drone into Forrest City that contained cell phones. Ricardo said,

"I was trying to fly it to a point above the trash containers behind our barracks where it would be picked up by another inmate, but a gust of wind caught it at the last minute and smashed it into the building. It broke into pieces and the cell phones were spread out on the ground. The guards found it the next morning and figured which group it was for from where the cell phones were purchased (The Shining Path). All of us got shipped to other sites in the prison system; I got Beaumont."

The next morning at 7:30 AM, Ricardo came into the UA barracks lobby where I and a lot of others were waiting for our morning work call. Ricardo had his "take home" possessions in a trash bag with him. Take home possessions are items that the BOP allows you to take with you. Take home possessions include, a religious book, any book you have had sent to you, up to three, your toilet articles, and any games, like chess, that you have purchased while in prison. Inmates recognize another inmate with a "take home bag" and a lot of them came up to Ricardo and shook his hand and wished him luck. I held his take home bag so he could shake hands with the inmates coming up to him to wish him well. The work call sounded, and Ricardo and I walked next to each other out of the barracks and me toward the Education Department and Ricardo toward the "I and O" (In and Out) Department. The sidewalk is common to both for about 300 yards. I could see Ricardo looking back at the barracks, the rec yard, the chow hall and at the hundreds of inmates walking with us. I asked Ricardo,

"Are you going to miss this?"

He laughed and said,

"I'll miss you and a few others, but no, I'll not miss anything else and I won't get back into the system."

I responded,

"I wish you luck and I hope you are right."

When we came to the fork in the sidewalk, I shook his hand and handed him his "go home" bag. He took the bag, smiled and turned toward the I and O Department, I turned and kept walking toward the Education Department. I hope Ricardo and Evelyn live happily ever after. Evelyn started flying to Houston to stay with her sister almost every month instead of driving from Kansas City to Forrest City — faithful beyond reason, I believe.

My closest friend at Beaumont Low for the period that he was there with me was Beau. Beau was the first inmate who ever said anything to me. He was the guy sitting on the top bunk across from me in the chicken coop who said,

"Welcome to Beaumont."

I had walked in and sat down in my assigned bottom bunk across from him. Beau was Cajun from New Orleans and was serving a three-year sentence for growing, using and selling marijuana. Beau was also a self-taught artist in watercolors and colored pencils. He had a job working for tattoo artists. They would have him sketch what an inmate wanted tattooed on their body. In some instances, if it were a really intricate portrait, they would pay Beau a portion of their tattooing fee for Beau to draw the portrait directly on the inmate's body. Then, the tattoo artist could just trace the portrait when making the tattoo. Beau, for all of his work around tattoos in prison, did not have a tattoo.

Beau was in his early thirties; not old enough to have been alive in the late 1960's but he seemed like a throwback to the late 1960's, pure flower child and beatnik. Beau had no one on the outside to send him money, so he made his money by doing portraits and assisting tattoo artists. Beau came to me one evening and asked,

"You take your laundry on Tuesday mornings because of your ID number correct?"

I said,

"Yes, I did, why?"

Beau asked me,

"Could you stop at the Commissary on your way back? You go right by it, and pick up the free hygiene products they have for inmates who do not have commissary money? I need more shampoo, toothpaste, and disposable razors then they allow any one inmate to have."

I said,

"Sure, I will."

After that, every week I would get the free hygiene products for Beau. I also picked up five sheets of notebook paper and three plain envelopes. The free stationery was provided so inmates who had no commissary money could write three letters per week using the five sheets of notebook paper. The notebook paper and envelopes supplemented my own supply. I used about five envelopes per week and about a dozen sheets of yellow, legal pad paper to write letters to my wife, my two sisters, and a few other friends who regularly wrote to me.

Beau came to me one evening in my cell. He said he needed advice for a personal problem. Beau had left his girlfriend in New Orleans in what had been his apartment. He had given his sister, who lived a few blocks away, enough money to pay the rent on the apartment for the duration of his sentence. Beau said that he had also asked his sister to check up on Gloria, his girlfriend, at least once a week while he was in prison. I asked Beau why he did not give the rent money directly to his girlfriend and why his sister needed to check up on his girlfriend weekly? Beau said,

"Gloria is schizophrenic from extensive drug use. She has medication to take for it, but sometimes she stops taking it because it makes her dopy. When I called my sister earlier this evening, she told me Gloria had abandoned the apartment and is now living in a city park in the French Quarter and sleeping either on a park bench or under bushes in the park. I'm very worried about her. What should I do?"

The first thought that came to me was,

"Abandon her; it is a losing battle."

However, I thought better of it and instead said,

"Can you ask your sister to get in touch with the Salvation Army or Catholic Charities? Both of these entities have a presence in the French Quarter because I have been there, and I have seen them asking for donations on the street corner alongside street performers. Perhaps your sister could take one of the men or women from the Salvation Army or Catholic Charities to your sister. Beyond that, you

should face reality that you and your sister can only do so much for her and hope for the best. Do not drive yourself crazy worrying about something you cannot fix."

Beau left to call his sister and ask her to do what I had just suggested to him. Beau came to me about a week later and told me his sister could not find Gloria and did not know where she was. It is a lose end to Beau's story. I will never know what happened to Gloria. *Such is the stuff of real-life stories...*

Chapter VIII
Odds

The most interesting character I met while in prison was a man whose nickname is "Odds." I never knew his real name. I was sitting in the barracks Library by myself about 7:00 AM on a Saturday morning reading a murder mystery novel one of my sisters had sent me. Another inmate walked in and sat down at the table next to me. He was a little over six feet in height, very thin with a gray beard and long gray hair tied in a ponytail. I judged him to be about 60 years old, and he did not wear glasses, but he did wear a kippah.[27] He had a large notebook and a stack of loose notebook papers heavily written on. We nodded to each other and I kept reading and he kept writing. About fifteen minutes later, he said,

"Would you like a really good cup of coffee?"

I said,

"Yes, I certainly would."

He asked,

"Do you like cream or sugar in it?"

I responded,

"No, thank you."

He left, and in a few minutes came back with two Styrofoam cups of coffee. Styrofoam cups are not

---

[27] kippah — also called "yarmulke" — a skull cap worn by Jewish men (and some Jewish women). Wearing the kippah demonstrates a reverence for God.

available to inmates and I wondered where he got the cups. I took a sip of the coffee and wondered where he got the coffee, it certainly was not instant coffee. He smiled, held out his hand for me to shake and said,

"Call me 'Odds'."

I shook his hand and told him,

"My name is Charles."

Odds started telling me his story.[28] I never figured out if it is normal for inmates who have just met to exchange their stories. Or, if it was just me, and that for some reason, inmates wanted me to know why they were in federal prison.

Odds was from Israel and had a PhD in Mathematics from Columbia University in New York and a master's degree in mathematics from the University of Haifa in Israel. Odds was serving a life sentence for espionage against the United States on behalf of Israel. That fact was surreal to me. I did not know close allies — especially Israel — would spy on the United States. Odds was a fighter pilot, a colonel, in the Israeli Air Force. He never told me exactly what he was trying to find, but I know it was some kind of technology related to aircraft weaponry. I told him my story. The fact that my story was military related, and that I was an engineer with two master's degrees, seemed to impress Odds.

I asked Odds what all the paperwork was about. Odds told me that his nickname of "Odds" was because he was the guy for all of the prisons at Beaumont that set the odds for sporting events that

---

[28] an inmate's story — in the prison context it is how he got to federal prison

were going to have a lot of betting taking place. Odds told me there was a system in place that allowed betting to occur with large amounts of cash. The system consisted of outside support for an inmate that was into betting. The bet would be placed, and the loser would call his outside support partner to transfer the amount of money he had lost to the winner's account, which was managed by the winner's outside support.

Failure to pay off debts in a timely manner was met, as usual, with a night or shower visit by the enforcers for a particular barracks. The only alternative for an inmate in so much debt that they could not pay was to request admittance to the SHU for the remainder of their sentence. Transfer to another federal prison was not an option. The long arm of the cartel or gang that you owed money to extended throughout the federal prison system. The cartel or gang would already have members at whatever federal prison to which you were transferred.

Odds seemed to like the fact that he had in me someone who was technically educated to talk "shop" to. Odds calculated the odds to sporting events by this method and data:

- i) the win/loss record of the last three games played by both teams,
- ii) the win/loss record of the home team playing in their home stadium for their last 12 games,
- iii) the win/loss record of the visiting team playing in the visiting stadium for their last 12 games,
- iv) the point spread that each team won or lost over their last three games, and
- v) Knowledge of whether a key player was on the injured reserve list for either team.

I was impressed because Odds did not have access to a computer. A computer with Excel can do this calculation in milliseconds and the only thing you would have to do is input the data. Odds had to do the calculations by hand with the assistance of a simple four function calculator.[29] All of this data was plugged into this formula:

$$Pa = 1 - \left(\frac{Ga - Gb}{Ga + Gb} * 0.33 + \frac{Pa - Pb}{Pa + Pb} * 0.33 + \frac{Fa - Fb}{Fa + Fb} * 0.33 - N\right)$$

$$Oa = \frac{Pa}{1 - Pa}$$

$$Pb = 1 - Pa \qquad Ob = \frac{Pb}{1-Pb}$$

Where:
Team "a" is the home team. Team "b" is the visiting team.
Ga = Games won by Team "a" over last 3 games
Gb = Games won by Team "b" over last 3 games
Fa = Fraction of games won by Team "a" at home over last 12 games, including last season, if applicable
Fb = Fraction of games won by Team "b" while visiting over last 12 games, including last season, if applicable
N = if a key player was injured, 0.25 is deducted from the probability of winning. If no key player is injured, zero (0) is deducted from the probability of winning.
Pa = Probability of Team "a" Winning
Oa = Odds of Team "a" winning
Pb = Probability of Team "b" winning
Ob = Odds of Team "b" winning

---

[29]four function calculator — a calculator that only does addition, subtraction, multiplication and division. There are calculators that perform statistical functions, but calculators with statistical functions were not available to inmates. I wondered why, if Odds could get a decent cup of coffee in Styrofoam cups, he could not obtain a decent calculator, but I never asked.

Odds said,

"This formula is my own invention and I am correct for football and baseball about 75 percent of the time. That is better than the Las Vegas odds makers who are correct about 65 percent of the time for pro-football and baseball."

Odds was one of the most revered inmates in the entire Beaumont prison complex. I copied the formula and methodology down and sent it home in a letter to my wife. If I ever bet seriously on sports, I will utilize this formula. I have even adapted it for horse racing or greyhound racing, but I have never tried it. I could continue to provide examples, but I have included just one below for those who might be interested in trying it. Since this book is not a book on betting and statistical odds and probability, I will limit it to this one example.

Probability and odds calculation for an NFL football game between the New York Giants (home team), and the Arizona Cardinals (visiting team)...

Teams	***Games Won****	***Avg. Point Spread****	***Fraction Won*****	***Key Player Injury (Yes or No)******
Giants	*3*	*11*	*0.60*	*No*
Cardinals	*1*	*4*	*0.33*	*No*

**Last 3 games, including last season, if applicable*
***Last 12 games, including last season, if applicable*
****If Yes, deduct 0.25 from calculated probability, if No deduct zero (0) from calculated probability.*

Giants

$$Pa = 1 - \left(\frac{3-1}{3+1} * 0.33 + \frac{11-4}{11+4} * 0.33 + \frac{0.60-0.33}{0.60+0.33} * 0.33 - 0\right) = 0.59$$

$$Oa = \frac{Pa}{1-Pa} = \frac{0.59}{1-0.59} = 1.41$$

Cardinals

$$Pb = 1 - 0.59 = 0.41 \qquad Ob = \frac{Pb}{1-Pb} = \frac{0.41}{1-0.41} = 0.71$$

Probability...The Giants have a 0.59 (or 59%) probability of winning by at least 11 points. The Cardinals have a 0.41 (or 41 %) probability of winning by least 4 points.

Betting... Odds of 1.41 for the Giants to win mean that for every $1.00 you bet that the Giants will win by at least 11 points; you get $1.41 if the Giants win by at least 11 points. Odds for the Cardinals to win mean that for every $0.71 (or 71¢) you bet that the Cardinals will win by at least 4 points; you get $1.00 in return if the Cardinals win by at least 4 points.

I find it fascinating that inmates who bet lots of money on sporting events who have little formal education, and absolutely no formal education in statistics, can calculate and quote probabilities and odds for sporting events with ease using the formula developed by Odds. And they all do this with a simple four function calculator which is the only calculator that inmates are allowed to have.

Odds told me he almost never bet unless the event showed a probability of a team winning by a particular point spread to be greater than 0.90 (greater than 90% probability of occurrence). Odds would email his wife, who was living with her sister and her family in New Rochelle, NY and tell her how much to bet. He had made her a lot of money over the years. Odds and his wife corresponded daily, and he called her every Saturday.

Odds had served 17 years of a life sentence and one day, about six months after I met him, he walked into my cell on a Friday and said,

"I'm being sent home; I am leaving Monday. The US Marshals are picking me up, flying me to JFK Airport in New York where I have reservations on a commercial flight to Tel Aviv. My wife left for Tel Aviv yesterday to find us an apartment."

Odds went on to tell me his wife had been getting his salary as a Colonel in the Israeli Air Force all along because he was considered, as a prisoner, to be on active duty his entire time in prison. He was going to retire when he got back to Israel. I shook his hand and hugged him, along with about a dozen other inmates on Monday, about 7:00 AM just before I answered the Education Work Call. Odds was gone when I returned to the barracks about noon for lunch.

"You meet such interesting characters in federal prison" is an understatement in the extreme. In general, I found that inmates with the longest sentences, who were not also severely deranged, to be the nicest and most dependable friends. Others, in for petty crimes, are only looking out for themselves. Members of gangs and cartels are absolutely dependable. They live up to their agreements simply because the penalties are certain, severe and immediate if agreements are broken. The absolute learning is that you must pay your debts on time without exception!

Chapter IX
Prison Tattoos and Other Prison Jobs

Not having at least one tattoo in prison marks you as someone just not quite with the prison lifestyle. That is okay if you have skills that are useful to whatever group you find yourself in. And, having a useful skill, I found, is far more of a vehicle to fit in with the group then having a lot of tattoos but no useful skills to offer. As the barracks medic, I was called upon to provide needles for tattooing. I did not have a clue how to get needles, so I had to do some powerful thinking. I thought about it for a couple of days and came up with a plan.

Inmates who are diabetic have to go to the medical department to get their daily shots and they do not touch a needle; the nurse or PA (Physician's Assistant) gives them their shot and the needles go into a "Sharps Disposal" box on the wall. In fact, there is a Sharps Disposal box on the wall of each of the half dozen or so examination rooms in the Medical Department. I discussed my idea with Pablo, an elderly Hispanic man in the chicken coop who walks with a cane and who is also diabetic. Pablo goes daily to Medical for an insulin shot just before breakfast. Pablo's cane is Aluminum and hollow. The rubber tip can be pulled off with little effort, especially if a pat of butter is used as a lubricant on it just prior to walking to Medical to get the insulin shot. Pablo told me sometimes there is only one nurse to give insulin shots and she parks two or three inmates in one room and goes from room to room giving shots so there is a time when the inmates were in the room with the Sharps Disposal box but no nurse. We decided that when this occurs, Pablo must empty the contents of the Sharps Disposal box into his hollow cane. Just fill the cane and return the box to its hooks on the wall before she comes back to administer the shots.

Pablo had another inmate watch for the nurse, so he did not get caught. We also decided that it is even smarter to leave some needles in the box, so it is not apparent that it has been emptied. Pablo was successful on his first attempt. He emptied his cane in front of me and it contained eighteen used hypodermic needles — a bonanza for the tattooing business.

My first aid kit contained a bottle of isopropyl alcohol. I placed the needles in a coffee cup with the alcohol and let it set overnight with another coffee cup wedged on top as a lid. If that did not sterilize the needles, nothing would. The tattoo machine is actually a Dremel Tool that has been modified by soldering a ball of solder on the wheel, so the needle jumps at every revolution. Ink is obtained by putting standard Bic ballpoint pens — red, blue, black and green — in hot water and then pulling them apart and mashing the cartridge's ink into separate globs on wax paper, or an empty candy wrapper. Tattoo artists in prison are true artists, some of which made their living, at least partially, on the outside by tattooing. Anthony was one of the best tattoo artists in Beaumont Low and he also lived in the chicken coop.

The first prison tattoo I witnessed utilized four needles from Pablo's bonanza, and a photograph of the six-month-old daughter of an inmate in the chicken coop. I did not like the term "chicken coop" when I was in the ten-man cell, but it ceased to bother me when I moved out. Anyway, Rico is the inmate's name and he got two and a half years for illegally transporting aliens across the United States border with Mexico. Rico was part of Shining Path and had agreed to forego any pay for four trips across the border. After the fourth trip, his daughter, wife and he would get to cross as passengers for free on the fifth trip. Unfortunately, he got caught on his first trip. Rico missed his wife and daughter and was frightened for them and wanted a tattoo above is right breast of his daughter so he would be reminded of his daughter every time he looked in the mirror with his shirt off. Anthony only charged him ten books of stamps, half price, because it was a worthwhile tattoo. I sat on a chair inside the ten-man cell to block Anthony and Rico from being seen from the hallway. There were two other inmates in the hallway, sitting in chairs who were to give the alarm if a guard was coming. I had never seen someone being tattooed before. The whole process took three nights, about ninety minutes per night. Anthony quit each night when his hands got tired because tattooing is not an erasable art project. The finished likeness of Rico's daughter compared to the photograph Anthony had to work from was uncanny. To help the tattoo heal and the colors remain bright, Rico had to put hemorrhoid cream on the tattoo and rub it in really hard every night until he ran out of the tube of butt cream that was provided with the price of the tattoo.[30]

Rico had gotten word from another inmate that his village in El Salvador had been attacked by a gang and his wife and daughter had fled along with all of the young women of his village. If his wife had stayed, she would have been forced into prostitution. Rico did not know where his wife and daughter were, and he did not know if she knew that he was in a United States Federal Prison in Texas for two and a half years. Rico's plight really bothered me, and I actually lost sleep over it. What could I do to help him? I finally thought that if Rico told the chaplain about his wife and daughter, the chaplain, who was Catholic, might be able through the Catholic missionary system prevalent in Central American

---

[30] Hemorrhoid cream in prison jargon is called "butt cream."

countries to find if his wife and daughter could be located. I told Rico to go to the Chapel when the 12:30 PM work call was announced for Education, Legal, Library and Chapel. The next day Rico went and told the Chaplain of his plight. About one month later, Rico was called to the Chaplain's office and told that his wife was in a Catholic Charity house in Costa Rica and she had a job there and she and his daughter were safe and cared for. The Chaplain even had the mailing address of the Catholic Charity house so Rico and his wife could exchange letters. Sometimes, things work like they are supposed to work, even in prison.

Within the barracks, these jobs or services were common along with the prices charged. Since there is no cash allowed in the possession of inmates, prices shown are paid in either Commissary $'s, or US Postage Stamps at $1.10 each.

Job	**Commissary $'s**	**US Postage Stamps at $1.10 each**
Tattoo (typical 3 sessions at 90 minutes per session)	$264.00 (usually paid over 6 mo.)	240
Iron two shirts and two pants per week	$10 per week or $20 every other week	10
Wash sheets, pillowcase and towel	$6.00	6
Haircut	$10.00	10
Wash dishes	$2.50	3

Sweep and Mop Cell	$5.00	5
Go to Commissary for You	$5.00	5
Piece of Cheesecake or cake of the evening	$1.50	2
Glass of Apple Wine (8 oz.)	$10.00	10
(or any wine) Gallon of Apple Wine (or any wine)	$50	45
K2 (Synthetic Marijuana) toke	$20	18
Hit of Cocaine (called "Nose")	$150	136
Cell Phone (20 minutes use)	$20	18

One of the most highly valued jobs in prison is tattooing. There is competition between the artists, but they have colluded to ensure a stable market price for a tattoo. If you were a gang member, you had to trade within your gang unless the service or job you needed was not provided within your gang. Then, you can choose whomever you need in order to get what you want. Tattooing is not allowed so there has to be a lookout at all times while it was being done. Usually, in the cell in which the tattooing occurs, a celli would be on the lookout. Guards made rounds at two-hour intervals normally, but they randomly walk through in addition to the normal rounds.

At 4:00 PM and again at 9:00 PM, there is a count where every inmate has to be standing by his bunk as two guards come into each cell and count you, e.g., check your name against their register that states, for example, Charles Callihan is in cell 61, lower bunk number one (when I was in the chicken coop). Counts with inmates standing by their bunks has been implemented, I was told by an inmate, within the last five years. Prior to that, if you were in your bunk, but laying down, you did not have to get up. That changed when an inmate died, and his cellmate did not notice (or care) that he had not moved in a couple of days. It was discovered he was dead when the stench was noticeable in adjacent cells. I do not know if this is true, but it was told to me as truth, and having been there, it is believable. In fact, some cellmates would be together for months, and one cellmate would either not know or would forget their cellmates' names, e.g., they just do not care.

The tattoo artist who had a reputation in Beaumont Low of being among the best was my friend, Anthony, in the chicken coop. Even though prices throughout Beaumont Low for tattoos were the same, regardless of the artist, Anthony would usually have a waiting list and other tattoo artists would be wanting for customers. Apparently, this fact irritated one competing tattoo artist to the point that he shoved an anonymous note under the guard's office door that said something like Anthony in the chicken coop had a tattoo machine.

In response to the anonymous note, two guards walked into the chicken coop and trashed everyone's bunk and locker. They, of course, found Anthony's tattoo machine and accessories (ink and extra needles) and confiscated them. The guy who did, went from smart by eliminating the competition, to dumb when he bragged about it to his celli who did not like him. Word got back to Anthony, and since Anthony was part of The Shining Path, he complained to Senõr González.

Nothing happened for three weeks, and then one night when the guard was on his rounds, someone slipped an anonymous note under the guard's door that said,

"A guy in cell 73 has a stash of cocaine in his locker."

That is as serious a charge as you can get, unless you kill, or inflict serious injury to another inmate. Possession of cocaine gets you the rest of your sentence in the SHU, and if the stash is large enough or a repeat offense for cocaine, it gets you a new charge, trial and additional prison time tacked on to your existing sentence. In this instance, it got the guy who ratted out Anthony thirty-six months, his remaining sentence, in the SHU. They did not find his tattoo equipment in his locker, just cocaine. And, immediately after that occurred, Anthony had new tattoo equipment that looked just like the tattoo equipment the guy who ratted him out had. Prison justice is swift, immediate and severe if it is to redress a wrong done to a member of a cartel. Most gangs, and certainly not individuals, do not have the connections and resources for adequate payback, but cartels and some gangs do.

A typical inmate I came to know and like was "Shorty." Shorty was only in for nine months on a parole violation. He had tested positive for marijuana during a random drug check. Since he was on parole while serving a two-year sentence for marijuana possession, he was sent to Beaumont Low to complete his sentence in prison instead of on parole. Shorty had no family on the outside and therefore, no one to deposit money into his commissary account. However, Shorty was industrious and a hustler. Within two weeks of being in the chicken coop, he had an ongoing business. For two stamps, he would sweep and mop your cell. For two stamps per piece of clothing or towel, he would launder them in the shower and dry them by hanging them over the wall of your cell. When they were dry, you could put them back on your bed or fold them and put them in your locker. Shorty would also wash dishes or cook meals to order if you gave him the ingredients. Shorty took payment in either postage stamps, commissary dollars or food. I admired his industriousness and energy, so even though I sent my towels to the laundry, I would have him do towels and underwear and pay him in packets of dehydrated soup. Shorty served his time and I walked with him on his last morning with me going to Education and Shorty going to the In and Out Department.

Another inmate that sort of had his act together was Galen. Galen caught a twenty-four-month sentence for possession of cocaine, first offense. It had to be an extremely small amount of cocaine because of the brevity of his sentence. Like Shorty, Galen had no one on the outside to deposit money into his commissary account. Galen had a degree in psychology and was very eloquent. On the outside, he had been a salesman for a company that sells industrial equipment, like conveyor belts and bearings. The job he thought of, and it was truly original, was doing inmates' homework for a fee. A few inmates took college courses at Lamar University. Classes were held in the evenings in the Education Department in the prison, including the classroom I used during the day to teach GED courses. When inmates had a paper to write, Galen was the man. Galen was swamped with work, so he subcontracted some of the work to me. I could read a novel or write a paper on "People Problems in the Implementation of New Technology" in the workplace — 500 words minimum. I got 10 stamps which I traded for $10 commissary at my first opportunity. I learned later that I also got an "A" on the paper; it made me feel proud.

Another service I provided was to help inmates with self-study courses from the Psychology Department. If the charges against an inmate included violence, in order to be eligible for parole, these inmates had to complete self-study courses on anger management, alcohol and drug dependency, and control of depression. Some of the inmates could speak English pretty well, but not read English. Of course, the BOP at Beaumont Low did not provide educational materials in Spanish to the Psychology Department or any other department, except in the course, English as a Second Language. Wisdom and Government Bureaucracy should never be used in the same sentence. Inmates who could not read English well, or did not want to do the self-study course would ask me to help them, especially with writing essays. I never charged them anything, but I always checked with Galen to see if he wanted the $10 commissary and about half the time he did, so when he did, he helped them with the self-study course instead of me.

The easiest, best paying job in the barracks was the "lookout." Every day from 4:30 PM until lights out at 10:00 PM, Donald would be the lookout for the guard. His cell was closest to the both the entrance/exit to the barracks and to the guard's office. Donald's job, for which he earned $30 commissary per week, was to sit at the entrance to his cell and read a book but also keep watch on the guard's office door and the entrance/exit door to the barracks. Donald's signal, if he saw a guard heading towards either hallway, was to call out, for example:

"Eddy, come here!"

Every day the guy's name, or the callout signal would change and be communicated to everyone by a slip of paper with the callout message on it. The slip of paper would be placed behind the soap dispenser nearest the entrance to the sink in the bathroom. The intent would be that guards would not notice the callout signal if it were different every day, they made a random round in the barracks. Every barracks had their own lookout and callout and they changed daily by the same technique. Donald sometimes took the night off and whomever he picked to stand watch had to be approved by one of the spokesman for a gang or cartel. Donald would pay the lookout a portion of the $30 commissary he would get each week.

Chapter X
Fifth Graders with Attention Deficit Disorder

It became apparent to me early at Beaumont Low that almost all of my fellow inmates were not the upstanding, law abiding citizens with which I had associated myself for 68+ years. Some of my fellow inmates needed to be in prison for their own and society's wellbeing. In fact, some of my fellow inmates should not even be in prison; they should be in a mental institution for the criminally insane. I eventually found that some had been in such an institution but had graduated to Beaumont Low through the passage of time — their behavior and attitude had not changed.

As I recall from my youth, about the fifth grade is when boys (and girls too) begin to either feel superior or inferior to their fellow students. It is when fights or bullying begins to occur. A lot of the inmates I interacted with were still mentally in the fifth grade with no concept there might be a better way to think and behave. I did not realize when I took the barracks medic job that I was also taking on the role of counselor and confessor. I had to go almost weekly at the 12:30 PM sick call to obtain first aid supplies, including sutures and surgical glue, for my first aid kit. Unlike industry where you wanted an injury/incident report every time something from the first aid kit was used, at Beaumont Low, if the inmate could be treated from the first aid kit, it was not considered worth reporting, let alone investigating. This administrative attitude is not because the powers that be do not care about the health and wellbeing of the inmates under their care; it is because they have too few staff, and the really serious matters, such as arterial bleeding and broken bones, consume their workday. Therefore, anything that can be handled by the inmate/medic, and his first aid kit, is not worth reporting or investigating.

After the first six weeks of my barracks medic job, all of my pants had blood stains on them — not my blood. The prison laundry did not remove blood stains, so I had to explain to my wife and the friends that drove her to visitation that,

"Yes, it is blood stains on my pants, and no, it is not my blood. I am the barracks medic."

Events that on the outside would be handled by curse words between potential combatants, are handled with minimum cursing and maximum fisticuffs. As the barracks medic, I got to patch the combatants up and also provide counseling so I could patch them up instead of being the referee for another round.

For example, there is an ice machine in each barracks. The ice machine in UA barracks broke and there was about a two-week period between when it stopped working and they decided it could not be fixed and another machine had to be ordered. Therefore, UA barracks had no ice and to some inmates that is critically important because their food smuggled from the chow hall had to be kept cold to prevent spoilage (I never used even a single ice cube my entire time in prison). The door between UA and UB barracks is open between the hours of 6:00 AM and 10:00 PM so it seemed logical to those in UA barracks that required ice to maintain their quality of life that UB barracks' ice machine was available for their use. However, inmates in UB barracks who also thought ice cubes are a necessity to maintain their quality of life think of the ice machine in UB barracks as their ice machine and it is not available for anyone outside of UB barracks. There is also the practical fact that the ice machine in either barracks, even if it is working properly, is not big enough to supply the needs of both barracks.

It only took a few punches over about 30 seconds for the two inmates from UA barracks against the six inmates from UB barracks to figure out they were not going to get any ice from the UB barracks ice machine. What happens after the fight to the participants, both winners and losers, is that they realize that if the evidence of their fight is apparent to any guard, they are headed for at least a week in the SHU. Nothing says, "I was in a fight" like bruised and swollen knuckles, jaws and eyes. A bruised face, even with a black eye can be explained away by saying,

"I slipped in the shower; I was not in a fight; there was no body involved but me."

Yes, the guards accepted this explanation, even if slipping in the shower happened to the same inmate every other month. What guards would not accept is swollen and cut knuckles. And you cannot walk outside the barracks with your hands in your pockets, even if it is cold and you are trying to keep your hands warm. There are no gloves allowed at the Beaumont Low, Medium or Maximum-Security Prisons. Perhaps in the frozen north gloves are allowed but not in southeast Texas where a cold day is a day under 50°F. Invariably, inmates involved in fighting do not think about the consequences of their actions before the fight. It is only after the fight that consequences are considered, and their one and only hope of avoiding the SHU is the barracks medic.

What came to be known as the "Ice Machine Battle" occurred during my second month as barracks medic. I remember because it was the same day that Rico learned of the whereabouts of his wife and daughter and that they were safe. The eight combatants, even those from the UA side, descended on my cell, bloody and frightened of the looming SHU. The UA combatants, in order to return to the UA side had to walk in front of the guard's office. And there was dinner chow where there is always a guard at the exit of the barracks and another at the entrance to the chow hall. They all thought they were doomed to spend at least a week in the SHU (there are no ice cubes in the SHU).

I got out my first aid kit and suggested they get some ice cubes, wrap them in a towel and press it on their swollen knuckles. I explained to the UA combatants that their swollen faces and black eyes could not be explained away as slipping in the shower because they did not allow UA barracks inmates to shower on the UB side. They could not pass in front of the guard's office now. They had to wait until dinner chow call and pass to UA barracks along with everyone from UB barracks and the guard was at the exit of UA barracks to watch inmates exit the building to go to dinner. I suggested to the UA barracks combatants that they forego dinner at the chow hall and could wait in the communal shower, sink, urinal and toilet area of UB barracks for a couple of hours until dinner chow call. I also told them they should also put ice on their faces to keep the swelling down until enough time had elapsed that the, "I slipped in the shower" story would suffice. Those with bruised knuckles also had to put ice on their knuckles to keep the swelling down. Surgical glue in lieu of stiches sufficed on their knuckles for that evening.

Of the eight combatants, only one spent two weeks in the SHU. The next day, his instructor at Vocational Tech Auto Mechanics, where he was a student, noticed his swollen hands and cut knuckles and notified the guard. Since he was a repeat offender for fighting, he got two weeks in the SHU, instead of one week. Sam, the leader of the white guys, came to my cell that evening and thanked me for doing such a good job. Sam was sure both barracks would be locked down due to the fight, but since all but one was able to hide the damage, there was no lockdown at that time. The lockdown occurred when the guy in the SHU got out and met some UA inmates in the rec yard who wanted payback. This caused all of Beaumont Low to be locked down for two weeks, messed up my visitation, and the guy who just got out of the SHU, got back in for six months for fighting on the day of his release from the SHU. It did not matter that he was attacked first. The rule against fighting is,

"Everyone involved in a fight gets the same punishment, unless one or more are a repeat offender. For repeat offenders, punishment in the SHU is longer than for first timers."

Another month went by with routine first aid cases and the majority of them, surprisingly, were not fight related. One inmate got stung by a bee putting trash into the bin behind the chow hall. Another sprained his ankle playing basketball at the rec yard, and another injured his rotator cup lifting weights. I was beginning to think, perhaps no fights for a while, but no, the next fight hit close to home. It was two of my closest friends, Anthony (the tattoo artist) and Rico (the guy who got the tattoo of his baby daughter above his right breast).

There was a new inmate in the chicken coup, named Daniel. Daniel had been transferred from another federal low security prison and got my old bunk in the chicken coop. Daniel, on his first day, found out who to buy synthetic marijuana, called K2, and he bought some. Daniel went back to his bunk with the K2 and lit up. There is a strict inmate rule that you do not smoke K2 in your cell because if you are caught everyone in the cell gets the punishment.

You smoke K2 in the communal shower, toilet, urinal, sink area. Daniel did not care so naturally, Anthony and Rico, after warning him, jumped on him at the same time. Daniel fought back and knocked Rico out. Anthony broke Daniel's nose and also knocked the wind out of him. There was so much commotion, the guard came, saw Daniel and Anthony fighting and Rico on the floor, not moving, and called the general alarm. Eight large guards came running into the barracks and into the chicken coop. Daniel and Anthony were led out in handcuffs and shackles. Rico, though conscious, was taken out on a stretcher. Daniel was sent to the maximum-security prison at Beaumont (apparently, he was sent to Beaumont Low for fighting repeatedly in another low security federal prison). Anthony was sent to the SHU for ninety days because he had used a weapon — Pablo's cane — during the fight. Rico got one week in the SHU because everyone said he was knocked out with first fist thrown by Daniel which is impressive because Daniel was flat on his back in his bunk when they attacked him and pretty high on K2. The fight happened so fast and the participants led away so quickly that all I was able to do was stand and watch with my first aid kit in my hand. UB barracks got locked down for two weeks due to the fight because it was more than two combatants and there was a weapon involved.

A couple of weeks after what came to be known as the "K2 Chicken Coop Fight" was another fight that originated in the chicken coop. This one was between two inmates in the chicken coop, Rudy and Manuel. Rudy worked in the chow hall and therefore, was called upon to smuggle food from the kitchen into the barracks. There was a rule among workers in the chow hall that if you were smuggling food and they were expected to help by getting you the food to smuggle or keeping watch while you got the food, then they were entitled to a share of what you smuggled. This rule translates into the fact that you have to smuggle more food to pay your debt to those who help you. It is kind of like taxes in that you have to make more money than you would need to make if you did not have to pay taxes. Rudy smuggled eggs out of the chow hall, both raw and hardboiled. However, Rudy did not give any eggs or decide to pay off the debt he was incurring every time he smuggled something out of the chow hall. That outstanding debt caught up with him about 8:00 PM one evening while I was laying in my bunk in the chicken coop reading an Agatha Christi novel.

I was vaguely aware that Manuel, another cellmate in the chicken coop, was having an argument with Rudy about Rudy not paying his smuggling debt. Then, I heard Rudy say to Manuel,

"Hey! Just fuck off!"

Manuel, slugged Rudy above his left eye, and Rudy fell backward hitting his head on the bottom frame of his top bunk and landed cross ways on the bottom bunk. When Rudy tried to get up, Manuel hit him again and Rudy slumped to the floor but sitting upright. Manuel said,
"That's going to happen to you daily, not by me, but someone is going to slug you until you begin to pay off your debts."

I patched up Rudy as best I could. He had six stitches above his left eye, and it was black and swollen. Rudy did not ask me anything and I did not offer any advice. The next day when I got back from teaching in the morning, I was told that Rudy had gone to the guard about 8:00 AM and asked to serve his remaining sentence in the SHU because he feared for his life.

When an inmate leaves the barracks permanently, either by a SHU request or because he has completed the Beaumont Low portion of this sentence, his left behind belongings are "up for grabs." That is, the contents of his locker, even if locked since it can easily be unlocked, are sorted through and divided up. In happy circumstances, such as a well thought of inmate has served his time and is leaving, the inmate will designate certain items are for certain inmates. When I left, my cellmate, Chief, got my $10 prison watch. Harold, a longtime friend and former cellmate, got my radio. Others got my stamps and stationery. My clothing, uniforms and underwear, I gave to Sam, the spokesman for the White Guys. Sam is much bigger than I am and did not need my clothes, but he looks out for the White Guys and my size, XL, is common and someone would eventually need a pair of pants or underwear. Sam has an extra locker in the cleaning supply cabinet where he kept extra clothing. I knew Sam would put the clothing I left behind to good use.

When Rudy went to the SHU, I got all of Rudy's underwear, including three long-sleeved tee shirts that I wore under my short-sleeved uniform shirt. The long-sleeved tee shirts kept me warm in the barracks. It always seemed cold in the barracks even in July and August. When I went outside, I pushed the sleeves up and was as comfortable as possible in the hot humid weather of southeast Texas in July and August. I put all of his underwear through the prison laundry and wore them happily thereafter.

It is not surprising that the bad habits that got inmates into Beaumont Low came along with them. The habits or addictions are cocaine or K2 (synthetic marijuana), tobacco, or even pornography. The main addiction that I was aware of daily was K2. Bruce is an inmate serving a three-year sentence for burglary and theft to support his addiction to K2. He said he lived in a suburb of Houston, not far from where I live. Bruce lived with his mother in a trailer park. His mother came to see him on every odd weekend. When my wife visited, I would always see Bruce with his mother. His mother, from her dress and looks, seemed like she was addicted to something, probably alcohol and/or K2. Bruce came into my cell one day and said,

"I owe money to a lot of people in The Shining Path. I'm afraid that I can't pay it all back. Can you think of any way I can get out of this mess without going to the guard and asking to be put in the SHU?"

I said,

"Have you tried asking for a payment plan?"

Bruce responded,

"I didn't know you could to that."

I told him, that I would ask and set up a payment plan if, and only if, he would promise two things:

- i) he would stop, cold turkey, smoking K2, and
- ii) he would follow the payment plan until he had it all paid off.

I talked to Ortega about Bruce and suggested that Bruce could do members of The Shining Path's ironing and sweep and mop their cells. I already knew that Bruce did other inmates' ironing and swept and mopped cells to support his K2 habit. Ortega agreed to this arrangement and said the duration would be six months.

When I came back and told Bruce of the arrangement I had negotiated with Ortega, he was ecstatic. After that, Bruce could be seen every evening ironing, sweeping and mopping, including sweeping and mopping my cell. I had forgotten that my cell was included in The Shining Path cell block.

One evening while it was just Bruce and I, while Bruce was mopping my cell, Bruce said, *"Mom is proud of me for kicking my K2 habit and she told me to thank you."*

I said,

"Tell her she is most welcome."

Then Bruce said,

"Mom promised me she was going to stop drinking and hooking and get a regular job. She used to waitress at Antonio's [a popular Italian restaurant in his suburb of Houston]. She's going to try and get a waitressing job."

I just said,

"I sure hope she gets the job; she should join Alcoholics Anonymous."

I never asked, and hence do not know, if Bruce's mother stopped drinking and hooking. One of my many learnings in prison is that some people's normal existence defies my imagination.

During this time, the most surprising acquaintance, whom I thought was my friend and I could trust him, was Ronnie. Ronnie replaced Ricardo who moved to Bonito's cell when one of Bonito's cellmates went to a halfway house. The cell that Ricardo moved to was a three-man cell, but it had a window to the back of the barracks and a view of the forest beyond the barb wire fence that encircled Beaumont Low. As prison cells go, it was better than the one Harold and I shared with

Ricardo, and we did not have a window. I liked the location of our cell because it was across from the bathroom. Ricardo did not like the location because it was across from the bathroom and noisy. I have a hearing problem that is an asset in noisy prison cells because it was not noisy enough to bother me. So, Ricardo left, and Ronnie moved in.

Ronnie is 62 years old, walks with a cane and has very few teeth. He is also frail from a long-life of drug abuse, smoking and other non-healthy lifestyle choices. Ronnie got a place in the middle of The Shining Path cells because he had been a loyal cocaine customer of a Shining Path dealer on the outside. Ronnie also liked to smoke K2 and had a source of money coming in to always visit the commissary, pay people to sweep and mop out our cell (we had been doing that job ourselves before Bruce started the job) and to purchase enough K2 to keep himself happy in the evenings or so Harold, my other celli, and I thought.

One evening, Ronnie asked me for a stamp. The only stamps I had was from a "flat" of stamps (24 stamps) that had never been used. Ronnie handed me a blank envelope and I placed the stamp on the envelope and put the flat, now with one stamp missing back in my locker.

Two days later I needed a stamp to mail a letter I had written to my wife. I opened my locker but could not find the flat of stamps. Ronnie sat on the edge of his bunk and watched me go through my locker looking for the flat of stamps. I thought the flat had fallen down into another shelf in the locker. I finally gave up and said to Ronnie,

"Someone stole the flat of stamps I had; they are not in my locker."

I remember Ronnie saying,

"There is a thief about, keep your locker locked at all times and so will I."

The next afternoon because I was mad at whomever had stolen the flat of stamps, I vented to my friends in the neighboring cell that someone had stolen a flat of stamps from my locker and that it had one stamp missing on it.

The next evening after dinner, about a dozen inmates, including the enforcers, Ortega and Bonito came to my cell and said to Ronnie,

"You have a meeting with us in the TV room."

When I started to come too, Ortega said,

"This does not concern you Charles, you stay here."

I was shocked and surprised and had no clue what was happening. I waited expectantly and in about fifteen minutes, Ronnie, Ortega and Bonito returned to the cell and Ronnie was very red in the face and seemed very scared. Ronnie said in a halting voice,

"Charles, I stole the flat of stamps from you to get a K2 cigarette; I'm sorry."

I did not know what to say, and before I could say anything, Ortega said to me,

"We'll get him out of here very soon."

Ortega then turned to Ronnie and said,

"If you harm Charles or hassle him at all, they will carry you out on a stretcher to a better place."

Ronnie fell on the bunk and his face was now white and he looked at me and said,

"Why would they think I would try to harm you."

I said,

"I don't know."

After that, I pretended Ronnie was not there. I kept my locker locked. Even when I got my toothbrush and toothpaste out of my locker, I locked it, brushed my teeth, came back a couple of minutes later, unlocked my locker, put the toothbrush and toothpaste away and locked it back. Instead of reading in my bunk, I started reading in the barracks Library across the hall from the TV room until it was 9:00 PM. Then, I had to return to my cell for count. Ronnie just sat on his bunk and stared at the wall.

The next evening, just after dinner, Sam, Bonito and Ortega came to my cell and said, *"Charles, we are going to have a conversation with Ronnie, go watch TV."*

I left the cell and went to the TV room. About fifteen minutes later, Sam came into the TV room, nodded to me, and sat down and started watching TV. I figured, whatever it was, was over so I got up and started walking back to my cell. When I got to the barracks lobby, I saw Ronnie with his cane standing by the locked entrance/exit doors to the barracks. I heard the guard in his office say,

"Okay, I'll handle it from here now get out of my office."

Ortega and Bonito walked out of the guard's office and as they walked by me, Ortega said,

"Ronnie went to the guard and said he was a thief and that he had stolen a flat of stamps from you and wanted to go to the SHU."

Just then the guard came out of his office, unlocked the barracks door and left for the SHU with Ronnie. I went back to the TV room and asked Sam,

"How were you so sure Ronnie had stolen the stamps?"

Sam said,

"Because Ronnie had been trying to sell a flat of stamps with one stamp missing to the same people you told that someone had stolen a flat of stamps from you with one stamp missing. Ronnie's light bulb in his brain is not too bright."

So, it was just Harold and me in our three-man cell. I did not hear anything about Ronnie for about a month and then on a Friday at 2:45 PM when I was walking back to the barracks from teaching/tutoring, the loudspeaker said,

"Charles Callihan report to the Lieutenant's Office after the 4:00 PM count."

Usually, when you are ordered to report to the Lieutenant's Office you have done something wrong and the Lieutenant is going to tell you how many days in the SHU you are going to serve and when it is to start and also how many of your good time days you have lost. I knew I had not done anything wrong and my friends were asking me,

"Why did they call you to the Lieutenant's Office?"

I had to tell them,

"I do not have a clue."

Right after the 4:00 PM count, the guard unlocked the barracks for me to go to the Lieutenant's Office. When I got there, the Lieutenant on duty, who is second only to the warden on duty, was standing outside his office. He asked for my ID and I gave it to him. He then opened the door to his office and motioned for me to enter and pointed to a chair by his desk and said,

"Have a seat."

As he walked by me to go sit behind his desk, he put his hand on my shoulder and said,

"You aren't in any trouble so relax."

When he sat down, he said,

"I want you to tell me about Ronnie Nichols."

I had completely forgotten about Ronnie. So, I told him about Ronnie stealing the flat of stamps with one stamp missing and trying to sell it to the inmates in the cells next to ours. I told him about me, not knowing that he had tried to sell the flat to them, told the same people I had a flat with one stamp missing stolen from my locker. The Lieutenant shook his head at Ronnie's stupidity. Then he said,

"Do you think that if Ronnie Nichols is returned to Beaumont Low, he would be in danger? Not from you, but from anyone who doesn't tolerate thieves?"

I told him,

"Yes, I do. Ronnie is fragile from a hard life. I'm 70 years old with a heart condition and I think I could take him if I had to."

The Lieutenant responded,

"I agree with you. We'll send him someplace else. That is all; go back to your barracks."

When I got back to the barracks, Sam, Harold, Ortega and Bonito were waiting for me and I told them what had been said by the Lieutenant to me and from me to him. That is the last I heard from Ronnie, except when I got back to my cell, on the top of my locker was a flat of stamps complete (no missing stamp). I never found out who provided a flat of stamps with an extra stamp to replace the one that was stolen. I did learn that in prison, if you have skills that inmate's value, and you charge them little or nothing for your skills, they will watch out and protect you. I put that learning alongside the fact that if you are in a gang or cartel and do your part, fellow gang members will also look out for you.

Chapter XI
Tropical Storm Imelda

On September 18-19, 2019, tropical storm Imelda dropped forty inches of rain on Beaumont Low and the other prisons along with the town of Beaumont, Texas. Beaumont's city water system was flooded. Therefore, the fresh water piped to the prison stopped. Bottled water was brought in for drinking, but the chow hall shutdown — no fresh water, no dishwashing and no cooking using water. That means the 1300 or so inmates in Beaumont Low (along with the other prisons at Beaumont) for five days got the SAME bagged lunches for breakfast, lunch and dinner beginning September 18th at dinner time. The bagged meals contained...

Breakfast —

fruit (banana, apple or orange)
cereal (Frosted Flakes, Raisin Bran or Corn Flakes)
packet of skim milk
packet of artificial sugar (Sweet and Low, etc.)

Lunch —

2 pieces of sandwich bread
1 packet of peanut butter
1 packet of grape or strawberry jelly
1 Candy Bar (Nutty Bar or Milky Way)
1 bottled water
1 bag of potato chips or pretzels

Dinner —

4 pieces of sandwich bread
1 packet of peanut butter
1 packet of grape or strawberry jelly
1 candy bar (Nutty Bar or Milky Way)
1 bottled water
1 bag of potato chips or pretzels

2 pieces of salami or ham
1 packet of mustard
1 packet of mayonnaise
2 slices of American or Swiss Cheese

Yes, dinner was the bagged lunch plus two pieces of lunchmeat, two slices of cheese and two packets of condiments. We inmates figured it out real fast. I must admit, it was better than starvation, but it got old after the first day. There was a lot of complaining, but I found I could trade peanut butter for lunchmeat, which I preferred. And, I had dehydrated soup, mackerel, tuna, chicken, tortillas and a jar of peanut butter, a jar of mayonnaise, Louisiana Hot Sauce, Fish Steaks in Louisiana Hot Sauce, Ritz Crackers, Club Crackers, more sandwich bread, and six apples. I did OK. I also had decaf coffee and creamer. The inmates that really suffered were the ones who could not afford the weekly commissary visits, because they were stuck with only the bagged meals.

The rec yard, along with all work calls, as well as Library visits were cancelled. During Imelda, some guards could not make it to work so there were not enough guards for all inmates' activities. Most inmates sat in their bunks and stared at the walls, a common pass time. Others watched TV or played cards, checkers, or chess. I got involved with playing chess with Denis (Russian mafia guy) and even shelled out $43.12 for my own chess set and vinyl "chessboard." You can order a good chess set or checkers set from the Commissary. I brought the chess from Beaumont Low to Leidel and finally to home. The chess set now occupies an honored place on the top shelf on my one-fourth of the closet off the master bedroom in my house. In addition to Denis, I also played chess with Ricardo and Harold, but I had to lose to them occasionally, or they stopped playing with me; I did not mind.

The lockdown that occurred during Imelda was bad enough, just because we could not do anything except sit in our bunks, play games or watch TV. However, the worst part of it was since there was no fresh water, there were no showers, no water for shaving or washing yourself in a sink, and NO TOILET FLUSHING! Think of 175 inmates and eight urinals and eight toilets that you can use but not flush...OH BOY! The prison authorities said in a town meeting,
"There are no porta potties available because private neighborhoods, hospitals and assisted living facilities are ahead of the prison in priority, and there are not enough to service them."

There is that special feeling again.

I happened to be standing next to the assistant warden during the town meeting and said to him quietly,

"If you would let us fill mop buckets with water from the overflowing ditches in the Yard, we could flush the toilets, probably two flushes with one full mop bucket. Either that or let us start relieving ourselves in the ditches. At least the water in them is flowing away from the barracks."

He turned to me and said,

"Are you serious? Would that work?"

I said,

"Of course, it will work. If you will let us, I'll prove it to you now."

He let us try it. I got Harold and a mop bucket and the whole barracks, including the guards, assistant warden and other prison officials who had conducted the town meeting watched Harold and I fill the mop bucket. I let Harold, who had his doubts, carry the mop bucket to an overflowing toilet. He dumped it in and, big surprise, the water "washed" the contents down the drain just as if it had been flushed. The water pressure was not what it should be, but the important thing is that it worked.

A bucket brigade for each barracks was organized and about one hundred inmates and every mop bucket and some waste baskets started being passed from the barracks to the ditch and filled and then passed back. After about an hour and a half the toilets had been "flushed" and living was not so Hellish and certainly a lot more hygienic than it was. I had been the guy in ditch filling the bucket for barracks UB for about thirty minutes when a guard said to me,

"Hey 'Old Timer' how old are you?"

I said,

"I'll be 70 years old in one month."

The guard responded,

"Get the Hell out of the ditch and back to the barracks!"

I did not argue because I was cold and wet. After the fifth day, the warden for all of Beaumont's federal prisons went around to all of the barracks and thanked us (the inmates) for behaving ourselves during the tropical storm forced lockdown.

It was within a month after Imelda, just when things were getting back to what smacks of "normal" in prison, that the next "event" occurred. The event, described in the next chapter, was almost entirely caused by the over-zealous reaction of prison authorities to clearly what can only be described as the action of one mentally unstable inmate in UA barracks.

Chapter XII
Riot!

After the two-week lockdown ended, it seemed like everyone was determined to stay out of trouble. And everyone did for two whole days, from the Friday the lockdown was over until Sunday evening about 11:30 PM. And this time it was both UA and UB barracks under lockdown. The reason for this lockdown easily falls under the heading, "You can't make this stuff up."

Hallway in a Low Security Federal Prison

On the Sunday evening after the two-week lockdown, about midnight, I became aware of a commotion at the end of the hallway toward the guard's office. There were raised voices of the two men and two women guards. There is usually one guard for each barracks so typically in the building that housed barracks UA and UB (downstairs barracks) and VA and VB (upstairs barracks), there would be four guards. In this discussion, the guards seemed at times, angry, unbelieving and/or laughing all at the same time. The female guard, Rosalee, that I had seen earlier in the evening that I knew was assigned to UB barracks, walked past my cell.

Clearly, she was on a mission and clearly, she was livid. I watched her walk down the hallway to Sam's cell, directly across from Senõr González's cell, and three cells down from mine. She got Sam up, and watched him get dressed. Yes, some female guards like to watch male inmates in their underwear. Then, she marched him back toward the guard's office. I wondered, what on earth has Sam done? After about 30 minutes, the supervising assistant warden on duty for all of the Beaumont prisons came into barracks UB and headed for the UB barracks guard's office. After another 30 minutes, inmate spokesmen for all of the groups, gangs and cartels in barracks UB and UA were summoned to the guard's office for UB barracks. I knew then it was as serious as it could get and that probably someone had either been killed or very seriously injured — boy was I wrong!

2:00 AM — April 14, 2019 — Sam came walking back toward his cell, which means he had to walk down the hallway in front of my cell. Ricardo and Harold, my cellmates, were asleep. I asked Sam what was going on, and Sam said,

"I don't know whether to laugh or cry, it's surreal."

I responded,

"So, what is it?"

I don't remember, word for word the exact conversation, but it was words to the effect that the female guard, Rosalee, closed her office door and went on her rounds about 11:15PM. There is one guard for each barracks 24/7, and at two-hour intervals each guard makes a round of all four barracks. So, for about fifteen minutes, there is no guard in a particular barracks. The pattern of walking the rounds is random so it is never certain when a guard will walk past, or into, your cell. When

Rosalee returned from her rounds and put her hand on the doorknob of her office, it was sticky and when she put her hand to her nose and smelled it, she realized it was semen! Apparently, Rosalee knows what semen smells like and she is not married. When she opened the office door, there was a note that had been shoved under the door that said in elegant script,

"Thinking of you . . . Love, Your Secret Admirer."

Rosalee called the other guards on duty; they came to her office and after some discussion, they called an inmate orderly from UB barracks and had him clean the doorknob and door. They also called the assistant warden who was on duty and she came to UB barracks to discuss what to do about it. The assistant warden summoned all the spokesmen for all of the cartels, gangs and groups in barracks UB and UA to the UB barracks guard's office. They knew the culprit had to be in either UB or UA barracks because these two barracks are the only ones with access to her office while she was on her rounds.

After further discussion with the spokesman from the cartels, gangs and groups, the assistant warden said,

"UA and UB barracks are under lockdown until the guilty party comes forward effective tomorrow morning at 6:00 AM."

I said to Sam,

"We are back on lockdown indefinitely because an inmate has a crush on a guard, and communicated it to her in an inappropriate manner?"

"Pretty much,"

Sam replied.

I did the only thing I could think of to do, I went to sleep.

The next morning the usual loudspeaker awake up call was replaced with,

"UA and UB barracks are under lockdown until further notice..."

The announcement went on to say that sick call and diabetic calls for UA and UB barracks would be handled inhouse until further notice. Inhouse means that medical staff comes to the barracks for sick call and to give insulin shots instead of inmates walking to medical. Word quickly spread from the spokesman for each group what had transpired the night before to the entire populations of UA and UB barracks as well as the rest of Beaumont Low. The reaction from the inmates ran in equal parts the gamut from laughter, to incredulous, to anger, to rage.

A couple of days went by and word got to Sam from his counterpart in VA barracks that they had found the culprit. The culprit's celli had ratted him out to the spokesman for the White Guys in VA barracks. The culprit was, of course, a white guy, not gang affiliated. Sam, with the enforcers, Ortega and Bonito, visited the culprit's cell to try to convince him to confess his vicious crime. The culprit, his name is Ralph, after a few minutes of reasoned conversation with Ortega and Bonito, went to the guard's office in VA barracks and confessed. The problem with Ralph's confession was that Ralph did so with a broken nose and no front teeth, plus he was bleeding profusely from a cut on his forehead. Further discussion ensued between the guards on duty and the assistant warden on duty. Finally, it was decided to accept Ralph's confession, because it seemed genuine, and put him in the SHU for the duration of his sentence at Beaumont Low which was about nine months. It was also decided to continue the lockdown of UA and UB barracks because, obviously, Ralph had been in a fight.

From the inmates' point of view, the prison authorities had said,

"The lockdown of UA and UB barracks will continue until the culprit confesses."

The culprit had confessed, and the authorities went back on their word by keeping the lockdown in place. It did not matter to the inmates that Ralph had been beaten into making his confession. Afterall, prison authorities had not said the culprit had to confess without being beaten up beforehand.

The lockdown went on for a week. I lost a visitation weekend and ran out of books to read from the small stash in the barracks Library. I was reduced to looking through old biker and tattoo magazines from a Hells Angels gang member who was also my next-door neighbor, e.g., he lived in the cell next to mine. For the first time in my life, I saw pictures of girls tattooed in places that when they had their clothes on the tattoos could not be seen. And, from where the tattoos are located, it had to be extra painful to get them there — who knew?

After about a week in lockdown, Sam called a meeting of the White Guys. The meeting took place in our TV room. The spokesmen for all of the groups in UA and UB barracks had met and decided to go on a hunger strike. That means, no one answers chow call and chow hall workers, and medical orderlies (the only jobs that continue during a lockdown) would not respond to their daily work calls. Those of us who had food in our lockers needed to start sharing our food, e.g., those of us who had money enough to not eat at the chow hall very often or at all, needed to share food with those who only ate at the chow hall. The hunger strike would commence at the next chow call, which was dinner. Chow call came and no one responded. The guards at first did not know what was going on and called the assistant warden on duty. The assistant warden called the barracks inmates' spokesman to the UA guard's office to find out what was going on. Nothing happened for about a week, and I began to no longer find it amusing because I had run out of food in my locker. I should not have worried because the day I ran out of food is when the event occurred that made the hunger strike all worthwhile, besides giving me more material for this book.

The assistant warden on duty that day is what is described in prison jargon as a "Hard Ass." He liked to throw his weight around. So, during a stroll through UB barracks, he decided to make the lockdown even more of a lockdown by making all inmates stay in their cells and requiring them to call out to the guard when they needed to go to the bathroom or take a shower. The Hard Ass had three extra guards positioned: one at each end of the hallway to the communal showers, toilets, urinals and sinks and another at the entrance to them. This extra measure of discipline was the tipping point. Quick conversations from cell to cell resulted in the inmate decision to ignore these additional requirements. Inmates already knew the SHU for Beaumont Low was completely full of inmates from fights that had occurred during the lockdown from just UA and UB barracks. They had nowhere to put additional inmates who violated any rule. Inmates congregated outside cells and went in groups to take showers or use toilets, urinals or sinks. The guards positioned in the hallways and at the entrance to the communal area did not like the additional rules either, so they just looked the other way. The assistant warden was summoned to UB barracks. He literally screamed,

"All inmates are to return and remain in their cells!"

At that remark, almost all inmates walked out of their cells and stood in the hallway in clear defiance of his screamed order. I stayed in my cell and tried to maintain my casual observer of human behavior attitude.

To their credit, the Hard Ass warden and the guards, withdrew from the barracks. All the inmates cheered. In one of the few times I spoke up loudly in front of the entire UB barracks population, and said,

"Do not think we have won; they are coming back with reinforcements, probably including riot gear like percussion grenades and tear gas!"

Everyone got quiet but continued to mill around in the hallway and at the entrance/exit door to UB barracks. About two hours went by, and nothing happened. Then, from my vantage point at the entrance of my cell where I could see through the entrance/exit doors, I saw them coming.[31] Along with the Hard Ass assistant warden, there were twelve guards walking and three dog handlers, complete with dogs on short leashes walking slowly across the Yard toward UB barracks. The guards were in full riot gear: helmets with face shields, handheld shields, guns that shot rubber bullets and/or tear gas, bundles of plastic handcuffs and three exceptionally large German Shepherds on tight leashes. I yelled,

---

[31] The entrance/exit doors to the barracks have armored glass windows in the top half of each door.

"They're coming!"

Some inmates rushed to the entrance/exit doors, some went to their cells, but most just stood where they were and waited.

When the riot control entourage got to the entrance/exit doors they did not break stride. One guard in full riot gear opened the door just a crack and threw in a percussion grenade. Stupidly, I watched the grenade roll across the floor and down the hallway toward me with smoke coming from it as it rolled. It went off with a deafening boom and a flash. My ears were ringing, and it was like I had been looking directly into the sun for thirty seconds. There were screams and running as the guards rushed through the doors and inmates scrambled to get out or their way. I could hear the sound of the tear gas/rubber bullet guns going off as well. When a rubber bullet hits someone, there is a dull thud like a baseball bat hitting a watermelon. The inmate who is hit with a rubber bullet falls to the floor with another thud and just lays there, usually moaning. Inmates who had been hit with rubber bullets were quickly handcuffed and left where they were laying. The guards swept the entrance lobby in less than a minute and continued down each hallway. The dogs with their handlers came last. There was no tear gas, but the smoke from the percussion grenades and from the rubber bullet guns cast the barracks in a gray smoke-filled pall and it was difficult to breathe because of the smoke.

In about ten minutes, the guards were again in control of UB barracks and the Hard Ass assistant warden appeared at my cell entrance and said,

"Are you the barracks medic?"

I said,

"Yes sir" (I mentally kicked myself because I said, "sir").

He said,

"Come with me and bring your first aid kit."

I was led to the entrance/exit doors, and through the doors into the yard about fifty feet from the barracks. There were about thirty inmates sitting in the yard with their hands cuffed behind their backs, and there were four inmates who were coughing, and one had vomited down his shirt. The Hard Ass warden motioned to me and then pointed to the four inmates. I guessed he wanted me to tend to them, so I started with the nearest one. I did not know his name, but I knew him from just seeing him in UB barracks. He was African American, morbidly obese and I could see he had an inhaler in his hand. His eyes were tearing badly. Without me asking him anything, he volunteered,

"My inhaler is empty, I can hardly breathe, and I can't see because of the smoke."

I irrigated his eyes with a bottle of saline from my first aid kit and asked him if he had another inhaler in this cell. He said that he did so I asked one of the guards if I could go to his cell and obtain his inhaler from his locker. The guard said,

"No, you can't go, but I will go. What is his cell number and where in his locker is the inhaler?"

The inmate told the guard; he left and in a couple of minutes came back with the inhaler. Two of the other inmates needing my attention were elderly in that they looked older than me. Inmates who look older than me I consider elderly because I am not elderly. These two inmates just needed fresh air and after a few minutes were breathing fine.

The last of the inmates that needed my attention was young. I knew him well; his name is Jesse. Jesse had been standing in his cell when a rubber bullet fired at someone else hit the wall and ricocheted into his right hip. There was a tear in his khaki pants where the rubber bullet had impacted, and you could see his brown boxer shorts and a blood stain on them through the hole in his pants. Everyone wore light brown boxer shorts and khaki pants and shirts at Beaumont Low.[32] I had him take his pants down and there was a deep purple bruise on this right buttocks that had been bleeding where the bullet had impacted, but the bleeding appeared to have stopped on its own. Jesse said it hurt all the time but hurt worse when he walked. I asked him if he could walk to the Medical Department without assistance and he said yes. I had a nearby guard look at the bruise and asked if Jesse could walk by himself to medical for an Xray or whatever the medical professional said was needed. The guard made a call on this radio and said,

"Walk directly to Medical across the grass in a straight line."

Jesse pulled up his pants and took off for Medical.

Jesse came back with a gauze bandage on his hip, some antibiotic ointment and instructions to change the gauze every other day until it had completely healed. Jesse's problem was that he could not see his hip because, dare I say, it was his

---

[32] It was green khakis at the camp, dark brown at the medium and orange at the maximum. I do not know what color underwear they wear at Beaumont's prisons except for Beaumont Low.

hip. So, I got to change Jesse's dressing every other day for a couple of weeks. Jesse told me that dropping his pants for me to "mess with his butt" was the high point of his day, every other day.

Back to the riot...The inmates who were handcuffed were also stripped searched in the yard. Wherever they had been hit with a rubber bullet, somewhere on the chest or stomach, I got to look at it and press it to see if there were any obvious broken ribs. All were bruised and perhaps cracked, but none were broken that I could tell. The inmates also had a say as to whether they wanted an Xray performed — all declined. Since Beaumont Low's SHU was full, they were led away to the SHUs at the medium and/or maximum prison (no one I knew in UB barracks had thought of that). We were all ordered back to the barracks, but the "I have to ask permission to take a shit" rule was abandoned.

Among the inmates who were handcuffed and headed for the SHU was Beau, my friend with the schizophrenic girlfriend. Beau motioned for me to come over to him. I took a longer time than necessary to look at the bruise on his stomach from the rubber bullet so I could talk to him. Beau said,

"Please go to my cell, my locker is not locked. Get my tablets, watercolors and pencils and take them to the Chaplain. I think the Chaplain can get them into me while I'm in the SHU. Also, my address book is under my mattress. My sister's address is in it, her name is Cindy Broward . Please write to her and tell her what has happened to me and that I'm okay. I won't get stamps and envelopes for a week or more and if I don't call her Sunday, she will worry. Ask her to tell you if she has had any success with finding and helping Gloria."

I wrote a letter to Beau's sister, Cindy,...

"Dear Ms. Broward,

My name is Charles Callihan and I am an inmate in the same barracks as your brother, Beau. I am a friend of Beau's and also the barracks medic. Beau was caught up in the recent riot at Beaumont Low. He is all right, but he was struck in the stomach with a rubber bullet. Although bruised, he will recover completely.

Beau has been sent to the SHU (Special Housing Unit) and will be there for the next 90 days or so. He will be able to write to you, probably beginning next week, but he will not be able to use the telephone or email while he is in the SHU. Beau asked me to write to you so that you would know that he is okay. I also have given his art supplies to the prison chaplain at Beau's request. I believe the chaplain can get them to Beau so he will have something to do other than stare at the walls of his cell while he is in the SHU. Please do not worry about him. He is safe and being cared for, although the SHU is spartan surroundings, even for prison. You should expect to get a letter from him late next week at the earliest.

I was also asked by Beau to request that you see if you can locate Gloria and help her, if possible. I have suggested to Beau that he contact the local Salvation Army or Catholic Charities that I know are active in the French Quarter. Perhaps they would know if Gloria is using their food and shelter services?

I cannot contact Beau directly, but I can through the Chaplain. You can also write to the Chaplain. It is the same address as on the return envelope to me, but just write 'Chaplain — Beaumont Low' instead of my name.

Sincerely,

Charles Callihan"

Cindy wrote back to me once...

"Dear Charles,

Thank you for your letter. I was worried about Beau. He has been a problem for the family since he turned 13. I have always considered him a 'lost soul.' Gloria actually helped him become a more responsible adult. Beau had actually found someone in worse shape than he was. He has tried, as have I, to help her, but I think Gloria cannot be helped by either of us. I have tried to locate Gloria in the French Quarter and Garden District. Since I received your letter, I have contacted the Salvation Army and two local Catholic Parishes. Neither of these entities has seen Gloria and she is not in any of the parks I checked.

Since Gloria has moved out of the apartment Beau left her, I did not renew the lease. It is foolish to pay monthly rent on an apartment no one is living in. My plans are for Beau to move in with me upon his release in about 6 months.

I will write to Beau and let him know about the apartment, my efforts to find Gloria, and that you and I have written to each other.

I thank you for helping Beau and keeping me informed.

Sincerely,

Cindy Broward"

I did not see Beau again for ninety days until he came back to UB barracks with his head shaved, a beard and thirty pounds lighter. The first thing Beau said to me when I saw him was,

"The SHU has the best diet plan ever!"

I had to agree with him.

Apparently, when there is a riot in a federal prison, BOP officials higher than the warden must be notified. Also, it made local news because the hidden cell phones throughout the prison had been used to contact loved ones on the outside and the universal request was to contact local media outlets for Beaumont and report the details of the riot, why it had occurred and the BOP's response to the riot. This news even made Houston's media outlets much to the fear and consternation of my wife. It even mentioned UB barracks at Beaumont Low as the exact location of the riot.

Two days after the riot, still under lockdown, another assistant warden toured UB and UA barracks and there was a "town meeting." A town meeting is where everyone crowds into the entry lobby[33] and whatever official had called the meeting makes an announcement and asks for questions. In this instance, it was simple, officials from BOP regional (whatever that is) would be there the next morning to interview every inmate in UA and UB barracks individually. No questions were allowed and shouted questions at the assistant warden were ignored. The next morning arrived and at 8:00 AM, the officials arrived — three nice looking young women in business pant suits. Inmates, as animal-like as ever, cat called and whistled at them. They took over the Hispanic's TV room and guards went cell to cell taking three inmates at a time to be interviewed. The Hispanic's TV room was the largest of the TV rooms because Hispanic inmates made up half of Beaumont's prison population as far as I could tell. African Americans were next at about one third and the last major group were white with less

[33]An open space with a row of six computers on one wall and six telephones on the opposite wall between the entrance/exit doors and the hallways to the cells.

than five percent oriental, African[34] and Middle Eastern completing the population racial and cultural mix.

When my turn came, I was escorted by a guard, along with my cellmates, to the Hispanic's TV room. Inside the TV room. three card tables, each with two chairs had been set up, and they had been placed as far apart from each other as possible and still be in the same room. The lady at the table I was led to introduced herself (I do not recall her name). She told me she was going to ask me questions and whatever my answers were, they would be held in confidence except for BOP officials, and my name would not be associated with the answers. She also pointed out the tape recorder and said the interview was being recorded. My name was taken, along with my signature, on a paper that stated that I had been interviewed and advised of the anonymity of my answers to the questions and the fact that the interview was being recorded. The questions and my answers in *italics* are presented below.

1. Name and ID please?
   Charles Callihan — ID 19865-035
2. Your job?
   Education GED program instructor/tutor.
3. Why is this strike occurring?
   According to the inmates, if we gave up the guy who put semen on the guard's office doorknob and left her the note, lockdown would be over.

---

[34] African — I make a distinction between African Americans and Africans. Africans are black skinned, not brown, and most are Muslim, from Nigeria or Congo. Africans did not associate with African Americans except they shared the same TV room. Africans associated with themselves or Arabic inmates due to their shared religion of Islam.

Inmates gave him up and the lockdown continued.

4. Is there a gang or a particular group leading this?
   No, I went to a meeting and there were all groups, white, black and Hispanic all wanting to strike. I did not discern any particular group or gang leading it. It is a common effort.
5. Are you a member of a gang?
   No.
6. What is your view of this situation?
   I do not know the truth of the matter, but I know the perceived truth has united all of the inmates, regardless of gang or race. I want the situation to return to normal and, like anyone else, I want to be treated fairly. I believe group punishment for the actions of an individual does not work when...
   a. *some in the group do not or cannot use good or rational judgement (that's why they are in prison)*
   b. *the individual is not considerate of the needs of the group or any individual in the group*
   c. *the group does not know who the guilty party is*
   d. *regardless of actions the BOP takes, individuals in the group being punished must remain in the group even if they identify (rat out) the guilty party, and the consequences of remaining in the group after identifying the guilty party are far too harsh to make giving up the guilty party worthwhile*

   The BOP should already know this. In addition, regardless of why the lockdown is in place, it makes no managerial sense to implement "you have to ask permission to go to the bathroom" when you are already under lockdown. That is why the strike or rebellion occurred during the lockdown. It was not the lockdown itself that caused the strike or rebellion. If the BOP loses sight of this fact, and the assistant warden who ordered this punitive measure remains in a position of authority over the strikers, the strike will continue unabated or will cease, but re-occur at the slightest provocation.

She responded,

"Thank you, sir."

I walked out and wrote the conversation down as soon as I returned to my cell in a letter to my wife. That is why I can re-produce it here verbatim.

Since I had run out of food, I was really hungry. I had only had instant decaf coffee with creamer from noon the day before and it was all I had to look forward to indefinitely into the future. About thirteen hours later, Sam came into our cell with a tray of Nachos with melted cheese and Jalapeno peppers, and diced mackerel with sliced dill pickles, mayonnaise and Ritz crackers. All of us stuffed ourselves! I highly recommend this cuisine when you are on a hunger strike. It was the most delicious meal I had while in Beaumont Low. At least it seemed so at the time.[35]

---

[35] Hunger Strike — A hunger strike in prison, at least this one, was not a hunger strike in the usual sense. The concept of the hunger strike to the vast majority of inmates of UA and UB barracks was to stop eating at the chow hall and instead eat all the food in the inmates' lockers who were fortunate enough to have money for weekly commissary visits where they could buy food.

At midnight, during our hunger strike meal, Rico (the guy with his daughter's picture tattooed over his right breast) turned 26. He was still in the chicken coop but was on the waiting list to move to The Shining Path area of UB barracks. He was walked down to the cell next to mine by this cellmates for his birthday meal of Nachos, melted cheese with Jalapeno peppers, diced mackerel with mayonnaise and Ritz crackers, all washed down with coffee or water. During the festivities, the entire barracks broke into the Happy Birthday song. *Aha...memories...memories...*

The day after the interviews, the Hard Ass assistant warden and the warden over all of Beaumont's prisons were re-assigned. When the guard announced this during mail call, a spontaneous cheer arose across UA and UB barracks. And, the next day it was announced over the morning wakeup call that the UA and UB barracks lockdown was over, the rec yard was open as well as all jobs and commissary, and the email and telephone service would be operating as normal. If there is such a thing as euphoria in prison, this was as close as you could get for almost everyone, short of going home.

In the aftermath of the riot, more Sureños gang members were rounded up over the next five evenings in the barracks. The gang members who were rounded up were instigators of the riot to begin with. Rumor was that interview questions were geared to finding who the ringleaders were. These gang members were shipped to separate prisons in the federal system. No Shining Path members were moved anywhere. As a result of the dispersal of the Sureños gang, The Shining Path cartel moved even higher in the pecking order even though they were already first before the riot. However, now there was not a rival gang or cartel in sight. Senõr González was truly the supreme inmate leader for Beaumont

Low. I asked Senõr González once how he had pulled off getting most of the Sureños gang moved out of Beaumont Low and he just smiled and said,

"Old age and treachery will overcome youth and skill."

Upon reflection, Shining Path members remained neutral up to and during the strike. They were verbally supportive of the strike but offered no organizing and no inspirational talks during the strike. Leaders of the Sureños gang thought they were going to take over as the most powerful inmate entity at Beaumont Low because of their leadership role in the strike.

Old age and treachery will overcome youth and skill...

Chapter XIII
Simply Deranged

Deranged,[36] if you look at the footnote below, has a lot of synonyms. It is sometimes hard to tell if someone is deranged, but I had that question in my mind about anyone I ever had a conversation with while in prison, even with those whom I grew close to and trusted to a certain point. Afterall, they were in federal prison and I knew the charges against them because they told me what they were. Examples from my memory of phrases they used in describing to me what they thought of prison or life in general are presented below verbatim in *italics* as close as my memory provides. Obviously, I did not have a tape recorder and taking notes is not possible in what, in prison terms, is about an intimate a conversation as you can have unless you are gay, or bisexual.

Harold — Murder for Hire and Selling Crack Cocaine — 25 years to life, second prison term (also my cellmate)

Harold's first prison term was for possession of crack cocaine with intent to sell; he had served eight- and one-half years for that charge. He was out for four years and caught his current charges. Harold was back making and selling crack cocaine through a network. He could not make enough to meet demand, so he also bought crack cocaine from The Shining Path for resale. Harold lived in West Memphis, Arkansas. There was a rival competitor, not gang or cartel affiliated, that consistently undercut Harold's prices and sold a good quality product that the competitor made himself. Harold complained to his Shining Path representative when

[36] deranged — out of one's mind, disturbed, unbalanced, unstable, demented, berserk, lunatic, psychopathic, touched...

he had his bi-monthly meeting with him. At the subsequent meeting, two months later, The Shining Path representative told Harold to,

"Take out your competition."
Harold told Martin, his lieutenant/enforcer to do the job on his competition. The enforcer did kill the competitor but was caught and to avoid the death penalty, he "ratted out" Harold. Quotes from Harold...

"I told Martin to kill the guy, but I did not tell him to do it in a Walmart parking lot in front of dozens of people. What an idiot!"

"My daughter is doing ten years in the Tennessee State prison. She caught the same charge I caught the first-time in. I'm sort of proud, like father like daughter."

Sam (the leader of the White Guys in UB barracks) — Possession of marijuana and cocaine with intent to sell — 35 years, second offense for the same charge

Sam served 12 years in the Tennessee State Prison on the first charge and was out for six years before catching the current charge. Sam lived just outside Louisville, Kentucky. Every other month, Sam drove a van all the way to El Paso, Texas from Louisville. El Paso is just across the Rio Grande from Warez, Mexico. Sam would take $5,000 cash, nothing larger than a $20 bill, and buy cocaine and marijuana from The Shining Path representative. The cocaine and marijuana, purchased from The Shining Path representative in Warez, could be sold in rural Kentucky for $35,000 to $40,000 over an eight-week period. Then, it would be time to make another run. Sam's most memorable quote...

"I was so careful this time around. I knew I would not get caught because I always drove the speed limit, and I did not splurge on buying things like new cars and boats. I also stopped using hookers; they are awfully expensive, and they talk. I forgot that sometimes cops go undercover to buy cocaine and that's what got me this time."

Wilbur (he was called Wily Wilbur) — Forgery, first offense, ten years plus twelve months' probation

Wilbur is a real celebrity at Beaumont Low. He was on the run from the FBI for 34 years. Wilbur was the only friend I made at Beaumont Low that was older than me. Wilbur was 72 years old when I met him, and I was 69. Wilbur was in the mafia in Los Angeles, California. The mafia had connections within the city and county governments. For a fee, completed and on the record, divorce papers, waiver of child support, and waiver of alimony papers would appear in city and county records to the surprise of wives who did not remember a divorce filing or waivers of alimony or child support. The records, including notarized signatures, were flawless. Quotes from Wilbur...

"The divorce and related paper business was a gravy train. My girlfriend and I had an apartment overlooking the Oakland Bay Bridge. We had a sailboat and would spend the weekend sailing around Santa Catalina Island and eating at yacht clubs. We also had a Chevy Caprice that road as smooth as silk, and we would take it up to Lake Arrowhead and spend the weekend at a Bed and Breakfast above all the smog."

"Linda, my girlfriend, worked in the county clerk's office and had friends in the city clerk's office too. That was how we got into the business. It was really nice action for about three years, until the police and

FBI showed up at the county office where Linda worked. She telephoned me when they showed up and I said, 'Goodbye' to her and never saw her again. I don't know what happened to her."

"I hightailed it out of town by getting a job as a deckhand on a Sierra Leone freighter with identity papers I had forged for just such an occasion. The job lasted about eighteen months until we had a port of call in Marseille, France in Provence on the French Riviera. I jumped ship and got a job as a clerk at an import-export business. They liked the fact that I could get shipping papers for import or export so quickly. It was almost like I just made them up."

"I picked up the French language enough to pass for a native Frenchman after about two years, so I made up French papers, including a passport, and worked in a winery, and as a waiter. I even worked my way up as a headwaiter at Barcatalé's in Paris."

"Eventually, my fingerprints gave me away. I never could figure out how to forge them."

My favorite Wilbur quote...

"Adaptability leads to contentment."

Pablo — Transporting illegal immigrants into the United States – second offense – 5 years plus 5 years' probation (also a cell mate of mine in the chicken coop)

Pablo, the guy with the cane that obtained the syringes for tattooing, left for a homeless shelter in El Paso, Texas while I had been in Beaumont Low about four months. I was still in the ten-man cell or chicken coop and so was Pablo. Pablo had been injured in a motorcycle accident about 20 years before and had lost his right knee as a result. That is, his right leg was stiff as he had no knee joint. However, Pablo had been a truck driver all his life from the United States into Mexico and back. That was how he went from truck driver of regular cargo to truck driver of illegal aliens. There is, of course, more money in transporting illegal aliens than normal cargo until you get caught. Pablo has no money and no family, but in El Paso, his hometown, there is a home for homeless men and across the street an equivalent home for homeless women and they are operated by the Jesuits. Pablo had applied for this home and stated he was an experienced truck driver and was bi-lingual under the heading "Useful Skills." The men's and women's homes for the homeless in El Paso depend on donations of money and food. There is a restaurant, grocery store and bakery route that someone in a van makes to all the restaurants, grocery stores and bakeries in the El Paso area that are part of the donation program for the Jesuit home for the homeless shelters. Pablo got the job as their van driver and food pickup man based on the letter he had written to the Jesuits. He was ecstatic about it and I was proud because I wrote the letter for his signature that got him accepted to the home along with the job of van driver and food pickup man. Pablo's most notable quotes...

"I hope I can find a woman at the women's homeless shelter across the street. The women are mostly convicted felons like me so my prison background might even be attractive to them, or at least it won't turn them off."

"If I can live out my days at the shelter, driving the van and picking up food, and if I can find someone at the women's home across the street that I can talk to and be with, I'll die a happy man."

One of the signs of mental health is planning ahead and having a dream.

Denis — Human Trafficking – life without parole (also the guy I played chess with three times a week)

Denis had a successful "labor and immigration service." While we played chess, Denis would reminisce about life in Ufa, the Russian city in the Urals that was his hometown, and also his business base. I learned far more about the labor and immigration business than I ever thought I would while playing chess. Young women from Siberia, Russia, Ukraine or another eastern European country would sign up to "work abroad." Some of the women who signed up were already prostitutes so it was not a surprise to them what the "labor" was going to be after the immigration part of the bargain was fulfilled. Others did not have a clue or thought whatever it was had to be better than home, or thought it would be domestic help, like a maid or cook.

In return for "five years' service," the women, some as young as thirteen, would be provided with clothing and food along the way and during the five years' service. Transportation was by train, bus, van or car in groups of two or three women to the same destination. Most of the women had already been "paid for." That is, someone had seen their photograph which was a full length cell phone picture with their clothes on, but you could see that they were the right height for their weight and in most cases were pretty or at least had the appearance of having a pretty complete set of teeth. I never quizzed Denis about what happened to the women at the end of their five years of service. In fact, I never asked him a single question about his business. I just let him reminisce for I found that the more he reminisced, the more likely I was to win the chess game because he would lose his concentration.

It is a shock to most western Europeans, Canadians and especially Americans that what is considered in the West to be normal morals is not universal. For example, while it is a prisonable offense to engage in sexual acts with anyone under eighteen in most western countries, in the Middle East and Southeast Asia, it is quite different. For example, in Saudi Arabia, sexual intercourse is prohibited outside of marriage, but there is no minimum age for marriage. In most of the Middle East, the male who is responsible for the female, decides who and when she is to marry, and so long as the man can support her, taking more than one wife is the norm. In Brazil, Bangladesh and Ecuador, the age of consent for consensual sex is 14. In Thailand, the age of sexual consent is 15, and the age of marriage is 20. However, also in Thailand, with a court's permission, the age of marriage can be any age, including pre-puberty. While selling someone into sexual servitude is illegal in western countries, it is considered better than the alternative, or is considered the one chance at a better life in a substantial part of the world.

One should also note that in these great United States, total servitude, including sexual, was normal for African Americans prior to the Emancipation Proclamation in 1863. And, until the Civil Rights Act in 1964, African Americans were not the full-fledged citizens they are today. In fact, Black Lives Matter adherents would argue they still are not equal to white peoples' rights and privileges. Denis's quotable quotes...

"I helped a lot of women obtain better lives than they would have had."

"I think my wife — I still think of her as my wife even though she is married to my brother — is as happy as she can be."

"My brother is a truck driver and helped me with my business. I'm glad they passed him by when they were after me so he can assist my wife in raising our children. My wife divorcing me and marrying him has allowed me to stop worrying about her and our children. They are in good hands with him."

"My son is going to be drafted into the Russian Army in a year when he is eighteen. I think he should stay in because it is a job for life, and he would have a good pension. Besides, unlike the American Army, the Russian Army never fights any country that can really defend itself. We fight countries that can't really stop us, like Ukraine and Georgia."

Howard — Bank Embezzlement — 10 years, first offense (never found out about his length of probation, if any)

Howard worked in the Library and occasionally came down to my classroom and sat in just for something to do. Howard was articulate and had a great sense of humor. It seemed as if he was one of the happiest inmates in Beaumont Low. Howard told me he was a loan officer at a bank in New Orleans. He, along with a partner in the IT (Information Technology) Department at the bank, thought up what they thought was the perfect scam or hustle. It probably was, but like so many other convicted embezzlers, they stayed with it too long.

The scam worked like this. Anytime a loan calculation was performed on the bank's computer, the calculated result contained values far to the right of two decimals places to the right of the decimal point (pennies). The computer always rounded to the nearest cent. Howard's IT partner wrote two lines of code that would collect the roundoff "money" and place it in a file. Then, every time Howard authorized a new car or mortgage loan, the amount of the person's loan would, for a millisecond, include the collected roundoff "money" in the file that had been building from the computer's calculation of money paid or borrowed. The computer calculation would then add the roundoff money to the dummy account Howard had set up. Howard would check this dummy account occasionally and debit odd amounts from the file to yet another account he had set up in an out of state bank. Whenever this out of state account totaled a little less than $10,000, he would send it to a completely different bank in yet another state that had his real name on it.

Howard had amassed almost $4 million over a five-year period in the account with his real name on it before an audit at the bank where the intermediate account was located found it during a routine audit. His partner at the bank in the IT Department got five years because he admitted his guilt first, according to Howard. Howard's plan upon his release is to buy about a thirty-five-foot sailboat and sail the Missouri-Ohio-Mississippi River system until he dies. I never asked Howard how he was going to pay for the boat and the ongoing expenses of sailing on the rivers. Perhaps Howard had stashed away more money than they found when they arrested him? Howard's quotes...

"If I hadn't got greedy and stopped at three million, I would have gotten away with it. The problem is the longer it is that I didn't get caught, I thought the less likely it was that I would be caught. My partner, James the IT guy, had less nerve than I did. I should have listened to him and stopped at a million apiece."

"My wife left me. I don't blame her; I miss my kids too. It would've been great if I had gotten away with

it. I was going to surprise her by saying I had made $2 million in the stock market and we were going to move the French Riviera."

Mohamud — fifteen-year sentence for selling cocaine plus an additional four-year sentence for stabbing another inmate

The additional four-year sentence was served in the SHU at Beaumont's Medium security prison. Mohamud entered the chicken coop on the day he "graduated" from the Medium to the Low and was in the bunk above me for about a month. In talking to Mohamud I learned that his name used to be "Jeff." Mohamud changed his name from Jeff to Mohamud while in the SHU when he converted to Islam from Christianity (he had been Southern Baptist). The inmate he stabbed survived. This inmate had been stealing from Mohamud and other inmates for quite some time. When Mohamud confronted the guy, the guy attacked him with a shiv. Mohamud managed to get the shiv away from the guy and in the ensuing struggle, Mohamud stabbed him.

During our conversation, Mohamud casually mentioned that his wife was a prison guard. I asked him,

"How did you marry a prison guard?"

Mohamud said,

"She wasn't a prison guard when I married her. She got used to visiting me in prison and saw an advertisement for prison guards at the State Prison in Jackson, Mississippi.[37] *She also converted to Islam*

[37] State Prison of Mississippi — 633 North State Street — Jackson, MS 39202

when I did. I've got just five more years and we can be together again."

"Converting to Islam made my life so much better. I'm calmer and I don't feel the need to fight back. My life is set before me, and I'm content for the first time in my life."

John — 10 years in federal prison for running a "guns in drugs out" business in Nigeria.

John was also in the chicken coop with me for about three weeks. John was a very devout Christian, but he was also African. John gave thanks silently (prayed) when he sat down in the chow hall or in the barracks every time he ate a meal. In prison saying prayers before eating is a rarity and people tended to avoid him. The Africans avoided him because he was not a Muslim, and all others avoided him because he would attempt to testify about his faith to them at every opportunity, including me. I listened politely and respectfully to him and he never mentioned it to me again. Inmates always seemed to try to determine what "slot" you fit in the first minute or two upon meeting you and then write you off if it is not what they consider to be close enough to themselves. John's most memorable quote...

"Finding Jesus has made my life so much better. I know I'm saved, and I want others to know the joy of giving your life to Christ. I wish I had found Jesus before I got involved in the drugs and guns business. If I had, I would be at home now with my wife and four kids."

John said other things, but all are along the lines, quoted above. I find it interesting that both Mohamud and John found different religions, but the same peace.

Clearance — Fraud surrounding the disposal of hazardous waste — 15 years — second stint in federal prison unrelated to this charge.

Clearance was the only inmate I met during my time in custody of the BOP that had incurred an environmental related charge. Clearance told me that I was the only inmate he had met while in BOP custody that also had incurred an environmental related charge. We had a common experience, sort of. I did not know what was going on around me, but I suppose I should have. However, Clearance did it all by himself and it truly had a mark of genius about it. Clearance's father had served time for embezzlement he told me. I guess the gene of craftiness runs in some families genetically.

A chemical manufacturing plant (well-known name I will not mention) in Detroit had about twenty 55-gallon barrels of flammable and toxic hazardous waste to dispose of every week. Clearance showed up unannounced at the company entrance gate, complete with a business card something like this...

Clearance Perkins — Principal
Clarendon, Inc.
5501 Simpson Drive,
Lansing, MI 48901

Tel (555) 437-2957
Fax (555) 437-2956
cperkins@aol.com

Waste – Hazardous and Non-hazardous Disposal Services

Clearance's company offered disposal services at about one half the cost of the plant's current disposal company. Clearance guaranteed that once his company took possession of the waste, the company that produced the waste would have no more liability toward it. Clearance even had put this guarantee in their waste disposal contract. The legal department of the corporation reviewed the contract and readily agreed that it was a bargain too good to pass up. The contract stated that every other week on a Monday or Tuesday, holidays excluded, Clearance's company would have an 18-wheeler box trailer at their front gate to take up to forty 55-gallon drums of hazardous waste and the company was obligated to pay in full after every other pickup.

Clearance had another business card that looked something like this...

Clearance Perkins —
Principal
Clarendon, Inc.
5501 Simpson Drive,
Lansing, MI 48901

Tel (555) 437-2957
Fax (555) 437-2956
cperkins@aol.com

Inventory Control &
Logistics Management

Clearance had contacted six different warehouse owners along the riverfront in Detroit and leased six warehouses. The smallest warehouse, Clearance told me, was 40,000 square feet (almost an acre). Clearance also leased a forklift and placed it in one of the warehouses.

The scam was no simple it sparks of genius. On the appointed day, Clearance would arrive in the 18-wheeler with the box trailer (also leased) and pick up the forty 55-gallon drums of waste with all the necessary manifests that go with transport of hazardous waste. Clearance told me he knew the manifests were correct because he copied them exactly as they appear in 40 CFR § 40-45.[38] Clearance would take the forty 55-gallon drums of hazardous waste and put them in a warehouse he leased. When one warehouse was full, he moved to the next one until they were all full. Then, Clearance parked the 18-wheeler alongside the forklift inside the last warehouse, closed the account he had opened at a local bank that had accumulated $2.5 million over the five years it took him to fill up all the warehouses and left Detroit for Las Vegas. Clearance said he lived in a nice condominium while running this scam in Detroit. A lot of the money he made went to support his daily lifestyle.

After two months of one of the warehouse owners not receiving a lease payment, he began to investigate. He found the 18-wheeler and forklift in his warehouse and hundreds of 55-gallon drums marked, "HAZARDOUS WASTE — FLAMMABLE AND TOXIC." The drums also had the name of the chemical manufacturing corporation that produced the flammable and toxic hazardous waste. The warehouse owner called them up and asked,

"Where is my lease payment and why are you storing hazardous waste in my warehouse?"

Of course, law enforcement authorities, US-EPA, the Michigan Department of Environmental Resources, and the FBI all got into the chase. They caught Clearance because, although he was living in Las Vegas and working part-time as a blackjack dealer, he failed to realize that blackjack dealer's fingerprints that are required for a background check for anyone literally dealing in a casino, fingerprints

---

[38] 40 CFR § 40-45 — Volume 40 of the Code of Federal Regulations, Sections 40-45 — Provides the definition and management requirements surrounding the generation and disposal of federally regulated hazardous waste.

are shared among law enforcement agencies, not just kept with the Nevada Gaming Commission. Clearance could have gone anywhere outside the United States and stayed a free man forever. At least that is what Clearance and I like to think. Quotable quotes from Clearance...

"Why the Hell did I go to Las Vegas and get that job? I don't particularly like to gamble, even when it's not my money."

"I didn't think I'd get fifteen years for a first offense with no violence involved. I thought maybe five years at most."

"If I had gone to Monte Carlo, I probably would have gotten away with it, or even where I went if I had been more careful about leaving fingerprints."

My favorite Clearance quote...

"I'll still be under 50 when I get out. I've got time to figure out another scam and this time I'll keep my fingerprints to myself."

Adam — Serving three years for fraud — first offense

Adam is Jewish and a teacher in the GED Department like me. I talked to Adam every day during the week, and we became friends. Adam has a BS in Chemistry from Princeton.

Adam's scam ("hustle" in prison jargon) was "Kosher Sugar from Israel." I was surprised that his scam is illegal. I believe it was as surprising to Adam that his scam was illegal as it was to me that my colleagues at Explo Systems, Inc. were part of a criminal conspiracy.

Adam's scam...Pure sugar, imported into the United States, has a duty attached to it. This is so sugar farmers (sugar cane and sugar beets) in the

United States can make enough profit to stay in business. The result is that sugar that ordinary people pay for is more expensive than it otherwise would be if there were no duties on imported sugar. However, sugar that is an ingredient in another product, like pastries, is not subject to an import duty. Adam realized this was a loophole that could be exploited for profit.

Adam has a cousin who lives in Tel Aviv, Israel. Adam contacted his cousin with his idea. The idea was that his cousin would develop a route throughout Tel Aviv to just pickup, at little or no cost, day-old pastries from bakeries, restaurants, and vending companies. His cousin would put all the pastries in trash bags without regard to keeping the pastries intact or edible. When he had accumulated about 13,000 kilograms (30,000 pounds), he would ship them to Adam in the United States by the cheapest method available which is by ship as a partial container load. Adam would receive trash bags full of pastries that all contained sugar at two-month intervals. Adam would dump all the pastry "mess" into a tank of water in a 10,000 square foot space he had rented in a warehouse near his home in Queens, one of New York City's five boroughs. After a 24-hour soak in the water, he would decant the water which was saturated with sugar.[39] This saturated sugar solution would be pumped into a series of shallow pans that Adam had bought on Ebay from a bankrupt bakery. He would let the water evaporate and the result was a coating of pure sugar in the bottom of each shallow pan.

Adam would scrape each pan into a bin that was part of box packaging equipment that Adam has

[39]decant — skim the water off the top of the solid portion that had sunk to the bottom of the tank

also bought used on Ebay. The packaged product looked something like this...

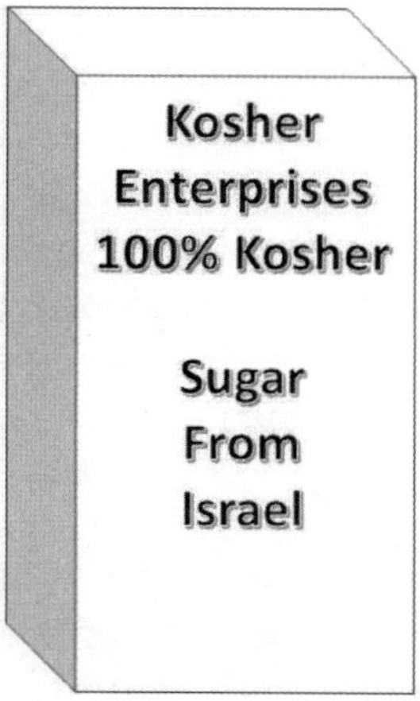

"Kosher Sugar from Israel" was sold in one-pound boxes in Jewish Grocery stores in New York City for a couple of years until someone (Adam never found out who) figured out it was not Kosher and notified the police. Adam's quotable quotes...

"I wonder what I could have done to make it Kosher. I don't know what the Hell 'Kosher' is anyway when it comes to sugar."

"Nothing happened to my cousin in Israel. I'm glad of that but why did they pick on me?"

"My wife thinks it's funny and we'll have a good story to tell our grandchildren."

"My wife and I are planning to open a Jewish bakery when I get out. She is going to the New York Institute of Culinary Art while I'm in here so at least one of us will know how to bake on a large scale when I get out. She'll handle the baking and I'll handle the finances."

Leonard — 25 years for cocaine manufacture — first offense

Leonard was a medical orderly and had been an EMT (Emergency Medical Technician) prior to going into the cocaine manufacturing and selling business. As always, manufacturing cocaine and selling it was much more profitable than being an EMT until you get caught. Leonard lived in the "unincorporated" section of UB barracks. That was a section between where the gangs and cartels were located and the SO section of the barracks. This unincorporated section housed inmates who were not affiliated with any group and who did not fit in with the White Guys because in Leonard's case his mother was white, and his father was African American. Leonard looked white to me except with frizzy hair that he kept just long enough to tell it was frizzy. This section of the barracks is also referred to as the "country" section. Each barracks at Beaumont Low had the equivalent arrangement to UB barracks.

Cocaine manufacturing requires the use of flammable and toxic chemicals. I will not provide the details because it would not be appropriate, and I believe the publisher would not want to put into print the recipe for the manufacture of cocaine. Another problem with cocaine manufacture is the laboratory setting in which it is made contains flammable and toxic chemicals. The higher the cocaine rate of production, the more flammable and toxic chemicals must be stored in the production area, and the space to house the operation increases in proportion to the amount of cocaine produced in each period of time. The larger the space, the harder it is to conceal and the easier it is for authorities to find. These facts lead to innovation in the manufacture of cocaine or any other illicit controlled substance.

How about putting the manufacturing operation in something mobile, like a van, and only be at the chemical storage site to load up the van for a day's production? That is the innovative approach that Leonard took. Leonard earned an excellent reputation for the quality of his product and his ability to deliver a specified quantity by a specified date. The day's production — about twelve hours' worth — would be loaded into the van. There would be a driver and Leonard, who handled the chemicals, ran the manufacturing process while the driver drove aimlessly around the Dallas-Ft. Worth area. This operation continued uninterrupted for about three years until the van went too fast over a railroad trestle and flammable chemicals spilled onto an open butane burner. The resultant explosion and fire caused the van driver to pull over, turn the engine off, open the driver's side door and run. Leonard had a fire extinguisher and managed to put the fire out while receiving first and second degree burns to his hands and one arm. However, the commotion alerted a Texas State Trooper who was driving by and who pulled over to help.

It followed that Leonard was arrested, tried and charged with manufacture of a controlled substance. The van driver had a previous conviction for a drug related crime and to avoid a thirty-five-year sentence, he "rolled" on Leonard. The case against Leonard expanded to include inter-state sale of a controlled substance, a federal crime. Since it was Leonard's first offense, only a twenty-five-year sentence in the federal prison was the result.

I met with Leonard weekly since he was usually the guy in the Medical Department when I answered sick call to get my First Aid Kit supplies replenished. Leonard, like most inmates, liked to tell people about why he got a bad deal and why he was in federal prison for a twenty-five-year sentence. He told me about realizing if he put dry ice in the box where the flammable and toxic chemicals were stored in the van, the fumes would be lessened, and he vented the box which was a converted Job Box used on construction sites to hold tools so the contractor did not have to take all of the tools away every day at the end of the workday. Leonard vented the Job Box to the outside of the van, so fumes were further lessened. He also had a ten-pound Carbon Dioxide Fire Extinguisher mounted near the butane burner and that saved his life when the fire and explosion occurred.

Job Box

Leonard's most notable quotes...

"I should have had the driver drive the van drive in the country on an interstate with long stretches of highway without railroad crossings or other bumps."

"My girlfriend bailed on me when I called her and told her I had gotten arrested. She didn't even try to see me in lockup. I don't blame her, I guess. Her fingerprints were all over the van, but she wasn't in the system, so they didn't come looking for her. At least they didn't know who to look for and I never ratted her out. I wonder where she is now?"

Arthur — twenty-five years to life, premeditated murder — first offense

I never met Arthur, but he was Harold's friend at Three Rivers Prison.[40] Harold, was my good friend and cellmate. Arthur's murder scheme is so ingenious I decided to include it because of the uniqueness of the crime and it certainly fits in the arena of "you can't make this stuff up."

Arthur was married to Kay, a mega-wealthy woman. They lived in a mansion in Dallas. They also had a 75-foot yacht at the Galveston Yacht Club and would charter a flight from Dallas to Galveston about every weekend during Yachting season which runs from mid-April until the end of October along the Gulf Coast. Arthur had long sense grown tired of Kay and hung out at their country club in Dallas as much as possible. Kay was happy with that arrangement because she would not have to interact with Arthur. Arthur also had a mistress. Helen, Arthur's mistress, when made up properly, looked surprisingly like Arthur's wife, Kay. This fact formed the basis of a "this would make a good movie" plot.

Arthur and his mistress, Helen, would rather live in the Pacific Palisades in California, than Dallas, Texas. Arthur could not divorce Kay because their prenuptial agreement would leave Arthur essentially penniless. As part of Arthur's and Helen's plan, Arthur began to tell his friends at the yacht club and at their country club that Kay had grown tired of Dallas and wanted to move to the Pacific Palisades area of California. Arthur told his yacht and country club friends that Kay and he were going to look for houses in the Pacific Palisades in a couple of weeks. Meanwhile, Arthur began to makeup to Kay by being extra solicitous of her and asking her out to dinner and for a cruise on their yacht in Galveston — just

---

[40] US Federal Prison — Hwy 72 W — Three Rivers, TX 78071

Arthur and Kay for an evening cruise in pretty weather. Kay fell for it, and sometime during the evening cruise, Arthur killed Kay, weighted her body and dumped it over the side.

Upon Arthur's return to the yacht mooring, Helen was waiting all made up to look like Kay. Arthur handed Helen, Kay's purse which included Kay's Drivers' License and their new life in the Pacific Palisades was waiting. There was no apparent murder, no missing person, no anything. Helen had practiced Kay's signature enough for it to pass normal scrutiny. Helen, now as Kay, accompanied Arthur home and life went on.

A couple of days later, Arthur announced to their country club friends that Kay and he were moving to California and they put their Galveston based yacht up for sale along with their mansion in Dallas. They bought an equivalent mansion in the Pacific Palisades area of California which is conveniently located 7 miles from Beverly Hills right down Santa Monica Boulevard, and 5 miles from Marina del Rey. They joined the Pacific Mariners Yacht Club in Marina del Rey to house their newly purchased fifty-three-foot Tiara Yacht and were among the club's most active and popular members.

Fifty-three Foot Tiara Yacht

Life was good until the unexpected occurred. Kay had a sister that had been estranged for years and Arthur thought the estrangement would last forever. Arthur could not foresee that Kay's sister would be diagnosed with terminal cervical cancer and in her last weeks of life would reach out to reconnect with Kay, her estranged sister. As soon as Kay's sister found out they had moved to California, she tracked them down which was easy. They were living in the open because they had nothing to fear. As soon as Kay's sister called "Kay" on the phone she knew it was not Kay. While Helen had mastered Kay's appearance and signature, she had no knowledge of childhood events that were in common with her sister. Kay's sister called the police and said,

"The woman masquerading as my sister is not my sister."

Local Pacific Palisades Police were notified and initially went to Arthur and Kay's house and asked her for identification. The identification proved to them that it was, indeed, Kay's sister. Kay's sister offered to provide DNA for definitive proof that the woman masquerading as her sister was not her sister. After three months of legal wrangling, a court order was obtained for a DNA sample from Helen. Of course, the DNA sample proved Helen was not Kay. Helen confessed their crime and both Arthur and Helen are serving twenty-five years to life in separate federal prisons. They almost got away with it.

There are no quotes from Arthur because this is a story I was told, and I like the story. However, Harold and I discussed this story and here are some of our quotes...

"If Arthur and Kay had disappeared by changing identities which they could have done with the money

available to them they would have gotten away with it."

"When people conspire to do something illegal, they should never feel 'safe' and always be on their guard."

"They should make a movie out of this story and make it so Arthur and Helen get away with it. They would be sympathetic characters if the real Kay, Arthur's wife, could be made out to be a real shrew."

Lawrence — 15 years for taking bribes – first offense

Lawrence was a former prosecuting attorney and was the absolute lowest of the low in status in the SO section of UB barracks. He managed to get into federal prison by shaking down drug dealers — taking bribes to look the other way or to remove or contaminate evidence — in order to fuel his gambling and hooker addictions. Lawrence would have this same status, in any barracks in any prison, anywhere because he had been a prosecuting attorney on the outside. Lawrence carried his burden with dignity. He kept himself immaculately groomed and worked out by running in the rec yard five miles every day he could.

There is an inter-community of self-help among the SO's, former policemen and prosecuting attorneys because absolutely no one else will help them. Inmate teachers, like me, would help them in class, but avoid them outside of class. I got away with it in the barracks only because I was also the barracks medic and I could, and was supposed to, treat anyone upon request. Since the "treat anyone upon request" order came from Senõr González, it carried far more importance than anything the guards could order. The worst thing the guards could do to you was put you in the SHU. The worst thing Senõr González could do to you was have you maimed and/or killed.

I saw Lawrence tutoring a SO in social studies one day in the Library. The SO was a student of mine in the GED program. Lawrence came over to me and very politely asked,

"Please, could you tell me how much social studies counts toward the total passing grade on the GED test?"

Since some version of this question was asked of me by students about twice a week, I had the answer readily available; I said,

"The GED test is divided into four parts: Reading Comprehension, Mathematical Reasoning, Social Studies and Science. In order to pass the GED, students must score at least 70 percent in each part, and each part counts 25 percent of the total score."

Lawrence thanked me, and I saw as I explained the GED scoring to him that he was writing it down. About a month later, I was awakened at 1:00 AM by a SO standing at my cell entrance and saying in a loud whisper,

"Mr. Callihan, Lawrence needs your help, please!"

SO's dared not come into our cell because Harold and/or Ricardo would attack them, but they could stand at the entrance of the cell and request assistance. I got up, put on my pants and shoes, grabbed my First Aid kit and went with the SO to Lawrence.

Lawrence was laying on his back in his bunk in great pain from his lower back. Apparently, he had slipped a disk in his lower back or aggravated a previous back injury. Fortunately, in my First Aid kit I had a box of "IcyHot Lidcoaine" patches used for muscle sprains and strains. I helped him roll over on his stomach and put the patch on his lower back. I also had aspirin and gave him four of them along with a glass of water. In about fifteen minutes, he was able to breathe easier and if he laid perfectly still the pain was tolerable. I told him,

"You should not walk the half mile roundtrip it takes to get to the mess hall and back. I'm going to tell the guard your situation and request they have a stretcher here for you at 8:00 AM. Stay as still as you can until then and have your cellmates help you to the restroom and back if you have to go."

Lawrence thanked me and his cellmates assured me they would help him to and from the restroom if he needed them to.

After this event, Lawrence, who hung out in the Library about as much as I did would nod to me and smile and keep his distance. We both knew that he and I would regret it if it was perceived that we had developed any kind of acquaintance beyond my job as the barracks medic. While Lawrence was letting the Lidocaine patch do its work, we talked, and this is Lawrence's story.

Lawrence was a graduate of Texas A & M University School of Law. He started out with a passive law firm in Amarillo, Texas. Passive law is a practice consisting of estate planning, wills, die with dignity papers, uncontested divorce, bankruptcy, and tax matters with the IRS involving no contest clients.[41] In short, any activity requiring the assistance of a lawyer when there was no adversarial matter involved. After about three years, Lawrence

---

[41] no contest clients — clients who were delinquent on their taxes but admitted it and were willing to institute a repayment plan within IRS guidelines

was bored with his job, his wife and his life. From a friend in the county prosecuting attorney's office, he became aware that the prosecuting attorney, a man in his 50's was undergoing treatment for prostate cancer and had announced his early retirement. The prosecuting attorney's job would be open, and the assistant prosecuting attorney was in line for the job, but that meant the assistant prosecuting attorney's job would also become available. Lawrence sent his resume to his friend, which was also his girlfriend or mistress, who had a secretarial job in the prosecuting attorney's office.

In due course, Lawrence got the assistant prosecuting attorney's job and life was good. There was not much to do if there was not a case and he could commiserate with his mistress during much of the day. About six months into the job, he was offered a bribe by a low-level marijuana dealer that had been arrested with just enough marijuana in his possession to be tried as a dealer and not as a user. He agreed to try him as a user for $2500 cash. He took the $2500 cash, and spent the weekend in Shreveport with his mistress, at the Lucky Dollar Casino in Shreveport, Louisiana which is about 550 miles one way from Amarillo. Lawrence eventually divorced his wife and became hooked on the lifestyle and never looked back until he was caught.

Serving time in prison is a degrading experience, but there are degrees of degradation. I experienced the least form of degradation, The Shining Path section of the barracks, while Lawrence was experiencing the worst form of degradation, the SO section of the barracks. Degradation by degrees also existed in the chow hall where gang and cartel members sat in their own area, while SO's and their associates sat in the area which is as close as it could get to the hot, steamy dishwashing and tray receival area. SO's and their associates also had to give up their seats in the Library and leave if a gang or cartel member wanted their seat which was often during the highest usage period which is early evening, immediately after dinner. When I left Beaumont Low, Lawrence was still eight years away from the end of his sentence and his back still hurt. Lawrence's quotes...

"Gambling is a slippery slope, you start it as a harmless pass time, like flirting with a girl in a bar. Before you realize it, the harmless pass time is the only thing in your life that matters."

"While I'm working out, mentally I'm not here. I'm anywhere in the world I want to be and I'm with anyone in the world I want to be with."

Elliot — Pedophile, purchase of minor for slavery — 15 years plus lifetime probation, first offense

Elliot was not a friend of mine, but one Saturday when I was sitting by myself in the Library reading Hemmingway's The Old Man and the Sea, Elliot sat down by me, and started taking to me in a low voice like he was my friend (he made my skin crawl). After about ten minutes, when I realized he was not going to go away or stop talking, I excused myself and went back to UB barracks and my cell.

Elliot lives in the SO section of UB barracks. He could not talk to me in the barracks because my cell was in the middle of The Shining Path cells. SO's could only walk through The Shining Path area of the barracks on their way to and from the bathroom. They had to walk with their heads down and say nothing. If they deviated from this, they would be punched, shoved and/or have their head scraped against the cinder block wall until it was skinned and bleeding. A SO was attacked this way a couple of times a month in the hallway just outside my cell and the bathroom which was across the hall from my cell. I could provide first aid to them if they requested treatment. On only two occasions did they request some antibiotic ointment and some tape and gauze for scrapes to their scalp and face.

Elliot approached me and talked to me in the Library on two occasions. After the second time, when I saw him in the Library, I would not go in. Or, if he approached me while I was in the Library, I would excuse myself and leave. What he said, I remember word for word. I include it hear because it fits in the arena of "you can't make this stuff up," and it provides an example of what significantly deranged means in terms of behavior and attitude. Elliot looks like Donald Trump. In fact, Elliot is a spokesman of sorts for the SO's and his nickname, even among the SO's, is "Trump."

Elliot, if you can believe him, is independently wealthy from family money. His father founded and ran a shipping company and sold it for over $100 million. Therefore, Elliot has a lot of money and a lot of time on his hands. I do not know where Elliot went to college, but he speaks like an educated man and carries himself as if he just walked out of a penthouse apartment on Park Avenue in Manhattan, instead of the SO section of UB barracks in Bloody Beaumont.

Elliot, according to Elliot, had searched on the internet on the Dark Web for a girlfriend.[42] Searching for a girlfriend on the internet, I suppose, is a pretty common occurrence, and in and of itself, is not something to be ashamed of. However, in Elliot's case, he made a connection with a man in

---

[42]The Dark Web is the World Wide Web that exists on darknets, overlay networks that use the internet but require specific software, configurations or authorization to access. On the Dark Web, I learned from my fellow inmates, you can buy human beings, military style weapons and ordnance, illegal drugs, hire assassins and even hire small armies of mercenaries to overthrow the government of a small country.

Thailand that for $35,000 would sell to Elliot a fourteen-year-old Thai girl. All Elliot had to do was pay half up front via bank wire, fly to Bangkok, Thailand and meet the girl and the man. The girl's passport and guardian papers from the government of Thailand were included in the fee. If Elliot liked the girl, Elliot would wire the second half of the money, and take the girl back with him to the United States to live happily ever after, and this is what Elliot did. The girl even spoke passable English and was happy to be living in a plush suburb of Dallas, Texas in the United States.

However, Elliot's neighbors in this plush suburb of Dallas, Texas thought the site of Elliot and his girlfriend, who looked ten years old, even though she was fourteen, and bowed to him like he was her master was somehow, not appropriate. The neighbors called the police and after a year-long legal battle, Elliot accepted a plea deal to avoid twenty-five plus years of confinement. His plea agreement is allowing him to serve fifteen years at Beaumont Low plus a lifetime of probation. Elliot's girlfriend (slave or wife), her name is Gan, was deported back to Thailand. Two quotes from Elliot...

"Gan really liked living with me and it's legal in Thailand. I did nothing wrong, the bastards."

"When I get out, I'm moving to Thailand."

I thought about suggesting to Elliot that lifetime probation probably does not allow him to move to Thailand. However, I did not tell him because I am sure his lifetime probation officer will inform him of that fact.

Chapter XIV
COVID-19 and Moving into Barracks WA

When the COVID-19 Pandemic was gathering momentum in January 2020, it became apparent from news casts that living near lots of different people was not a good idea. It also was apparent that since I was living in a federal prison with several months left on my sentence that I was potentially heading for an ordeal. The ordeal turned out to be worse than I had imagined.

I woke up one morning in mid-January 2020 to the odor of an outhouse. Since my cell was the closest cell you could have to the bathroom, it made sense that the outhouse smell originated in the bathroom. I got dressed, picked up my toothbrush, razor and shaving cream and walked across the hall and into the bathroom. The outhouse odor got even worse inside the bathroom. I was met by about a dozen of my fellow inmates who were all staring at the wall above the urinals. There was a steady stream of water that looked and smelled exactly like urine flowing down the wall, over the urinals, onto the floor, across the floor and into the floor drain. In order to not be standing in the flow of urine, you had to be up against the stall doors to the toilets on the opposite side of the floor drain. I got tired, and a little nauseous, of watching the "urine show" so I went into the next room where the sinks are located and brushed my teeth and shaved while trying unsuccessfully to forget about the outhouse stench that permeated everything.

I finished getting dressed and did not eat breakfast. I realized a good diet aid is to stay in an area that has the stench of urine and you will not want to eat anything ever. Instead, I went to UA Barracks and waited for the 6:30 AM Education Work Call. When 11:30 AM came, instead of going back to the barracks and eating lunch, I went to the

Library and waited for lunch chow call and went to lunch in the chow hall. I was hungry by then and I knew no matter how bad the food was, it would not have the stench of urine about it. After lunch, I went back to the Library and waited for the 12:30 PM Education Call and walked back into my classroom and taught/tutored until 3:30 PM when I had to return to UB Barracks.

Upon my arrival to UB barracks, I was greeted by the same smell that I had fled that morning. When I went into the bathroom, I could see that the orderlies had done the best they could to channel the urine flow to the floor drain. They had sacrificed four blankets and built a dam to channel the flow from the urinal side to the floor drain. There was a sign at the entrance to the bathroom that said, "Use the toilets for urinals" which needed no further explanation. From my vantage point across the hall from the bathroom, I saw the Lieutenant and Assistant Warden walk down the hallway and into the bathroom. They, big surprise, only stayed about ten seconds in the bathroom, then walked out of the building as fast as their legs could carry them.

Just before dinner chow call, the guard called a town meeting and announced,

"The bathroom problem is due to a broken pipe inside the wall on the exit side of the urinals from VB barracks on the second floor. VB barracks inmates are using their toilets as urinals and preparations are underway to tear out the walls of VB and UB barracks where the urinals are to make repairs. You must prepare to move to another barracks during these renovations. The move to another barracks for all inmates in UB barracks will commence at 8:00 PM tonight."

Not surprisingly, there were no complaints. Getting away from the outhouse smell was the overwhelming priority, and not staying in the barracks where some inmates had spent decades.

At 8:00 PM, guards started down each hallway with a list. When they got to my cell, they said,

"Charles Callihan, WA barracks, cell number 1."

That really surprised me. All the barracks are laid out identically to one another. Cell number 1 was Senõr González's cell in UB barracks. I waited in line for the cart that can carry all your belongings and about midnight it was my turn. I emptied my locker onto the cart, stripped my bed and placed the linens on the cart. We were told to leave the mattress and pillow because there would be a mattress and pillow in the bunk to which we had been assigned. I found out later that inmates we were displacing were being moved to SA barracks that had been remodeled but was not occupied until now. Some inmates from UB barracks were moved to SA barracks too. It would seem to make more sense to move inmates from UB barracks to the SA barracks as that would have caused minimum disruption for the inmates. However, I believe, part of the massive movement of inmates was to purposely break up clicks and gangs that form naturally in a prison environment. Of course, the guards never said that was a purpose of why they moved inmates around, but it was a result.

WA barracks was run by Indians. That is, American Indians, mostly from Oklahoma, but there was also a contingent from Louisiana. Chief (they called him Chief) was the leader or Chief of the Indians and my cellmate. Chief introduced himself to me upon my arrival with my cart at the stroke of midnight.

Chief has a loyal following of about a hundred inmates in WA barracks. No other gang of significance is apparent in WA barracks. Chief also runs the Sweat Lodge that stands beside the rec yard building. Every other Saturday afternoon, rain or shine, you can see smoke coming from the tee pee that is setup on the day of use. The wrappings of the tee pee are about two dozen blankets dedicated to the Sweat Lodge. The Sweat Lodge has a permanent framework of wooden poles visible every day but the Saturday afternoons that it is in use, and then it is wrapped teepee-like in blankets. The Sweat Lodge provides a place and time for inmates, almost all-American Indians, to talk to one another about their problems, seek advice and generally relax in a sauna like atmosphere. Wood is purchased by the BOP especially for use in the Sweat Lodge as part of the allowance of religious freedom required by the US Constitution. Chief also runs the leather craft shop in the rec building which is a popular craft for a lot of inmates.

Prison Leather Craft Shop (not Beaumont Low)

Chief, the night before I left for Leidel, gave me a wallet and a purse for my wife to remember him by; my wife and I use these daily.

Wallet and Purse Made in Prison

Moving to WA barracks was a great relief from the urine stench permeating UB barracks. I regretted being separated from inmates who had become my friends over the months we had been together. Now that I knew my way around and how to setup a network of services you want in a prison barracks, it took me about two hours to find a barber, an inmate who would iron two shirts and two pairs of pants a week, and where the TV room and barracks Library were located. I also liked being in a two-man cell for the first and only time at Beaumont Low.

A side benefit was being in the cell with the acknowledged inmate leader for substantially all of WA barracks. Chief, when we told each other how we got to Beaumont Low, said he was 18 years into a 35-year sentence and would be 72 upon his release. He was serving such a long sentence because on the Choctaw reservation outside Claremore, Oklahoma he had established a crack cocaine manufacturing business. Chief had been trained as a machinist in the navy and so he also converted AR15 rifles into fully automatic sub-machine guns.[43] It was the combination of making and selling drugs plus making and selling machine guns that got him his long sentence. The fact that two FBI agents were ambushed and killed on an Indian Reservation in South Dakota with machine guns he had manufactured did not help either.

Chief is also something of a gourmet chef in the prison barracks arena. He taught me how to make molé and I taught him about the Charles Stinger.[44] After I drew up plans for the Charles Stinger, four Charles Stingers became operational within two weeks of my arrival in WA barracks, another occurrence of which I am quite proud.

Two of the inmates I knew from UB barracks, Marty and Bobby, were next door in cell number 2, a three-man cell with the third bunk empty, while the Chief and I were in cell number 1, the only two-man cell in WA barracks. Marty and Bobby were cellmates in UB barracks on the other side of the barracks from where I was in UB barracks. They are not untypical of a small number of "partnered" inmates I observed during my stay at Beaumont Low. Marty and Bobby had been at Beaumont Medium as cellmates and had come to Beaumont Low from the Medium at different times with Howard graduating from the Medium to the Low prior to Marty's graduation to the Low. Marty found out somehow that Bobby was in UB barracks, he requested UB barracks and they approved it. Eventually, they

---

[43] AR15 Rifle — Manufactured by Colt Industries, it is the civilian version of the US Military's M16 and M4 rifles. It fires the 5.56mm NATO cartridge. The .223 Remington is the commercial version of the cartridge. The AR15 can be converted to fully automatic fire by a simple, 5-minute machining operation plus the addition of a lever that allows switching from semiautomatic to fully automatic or back at any time.

[44] molé — a Mexican American Indian dish made with chicken, milk chocolate and spices.

managed to become cellmates again in UB barracks. When they made the move to WA barracks from UB barracks to work at Unicor,[45] they remained as cellmates. Requesting relocation from one barracks to another is not unusual and is approved only for these reasons:

i) A job at Unicor which is only serviced by inmates in WA and WB barracks.
ii) Fear of reprisal from another inmate(s) and it is not gang or cartel related. If it is gang or cartel related, moving anywhere, except to the SHU, would not protect you.
iii) If there are very few inmates of the same race as you in the barracks you are in and there are more inmates of your race in a barracks you are requesting to be moved to, they will approve the move.

Marty and Bobby are friends, really, really close friends. One morning, about 2:00 AM, I got up to use the bathroom and noticed Bobby and Marty going into the shower together and it was not to smoke K2. On the door of each shower stall door in each barracks is a sign that reads, "ONE INMATE AT A TIME." Prison reality is that the sex drive does not cease while you are in prison, and inmates who are not gay, if enough trust is formed between them, will be intimate with one another and no one seems to care. I never saw or heard of anyone raped at Beaumont Low. It would be considered the worst form of bullying and is not tolerated. Inmates who form strong enough bonds with one another become intimate by choice. Both Bobby and Marty are

---

[45] Unicor — the main Beaumont Low prison business — making prison uniforms for Beaumont's prison as well as for other federal prisons. During the Viet Nam war, Unicor made army fatigue uniforms.

respected, and both are about six feet tall and 180 pounds each and both are serving 35+ years in prison. You can draw your own conclusions and judgements; I will not.

COVID-19 began to take a toll on the inmates at Beaumont's prisons just before I left for Leidel, the halfway house. When UB barracks finished being repaired, it became the quarantine barracks for Beaumont Low. Almost daily, someone would be walked or wheeled out of WA barracks to the Medical Department and then either to a hospital or to UB barracks. Some number of inmates died from the virus at Beaumont Low and the other Beaumont prisons, but I have no way of knowing how many. One thing the BOP is good at in any prison is keeping inmates uninformed of what is going on. The lack of information leads to rumors and inmates' probably thinking it is far worse than it is. Perhaps keeping inmates uninformed is a method of control, but it does not foster trust in the authorities who have control over inmates. A lack of trust does not foster good will or a willingness to follow rules.

Chapter XV
Visitation

Prior to the COVID-19 Pandemic, visitation occurred every other weekend. The weekend you are eligible for visitation is determined by the fifth digit of your BOP identification number. Even inmates have the fifth digit of their BOP Number even and odd inmates have an odd fifth digit of their BOP Number. My BOP Number is 19865-035. Since the fifth digit is '5', my visitation weekends were odd, e.g., the first, third and when it occurred, the fifth weekend each month.

My wife lives 94 miles from the prison but is legally blind, so she had to rely on friends to drive her to and from the prison. For the first three months, one of my sisters lived with her and they both would come with a friend who would make the 188-mile roundtrip on an odd Saturday or Sunday. You can have your picture taken with those who visit and with your significant other. Below is a picture of my wife and I that was made during one of the visits. Sam, the leader of the White Guys, took the picture. Sam's job is to clean and maintain the visitation area in good order and also to take pictures for those who want a memento of their time at Beaumont Low, like it is worth memorializing.

My Wife and I at Visitation in Beaumont Low

On the other hand, for inmates who are in prison for decades or life, this is their only opportunity to see in person and touch, however briefly, the love of their life along with their children. I was told this same story by more than a dozen inmates during my stint at Beaumont Low. Each one told me they had told their wife to divorce them and not wait the ten, fifteen or more years for them. Divorce allowed their wife to have a chance at a better life then if they waited until their return from prison. The only marriages that lasted decades apart from each other were the ones where they were both in prison, though at different locations.

I wore the uniform in the picture for the eighteen months I was at Beaumont Low. Consequently, I made a vow that I would never wear khakis again, and I had my wife throw away the four pairs of khaki pants that were in my closet at home before I returned.

During visitation, you could see all kinds of stories playing out in front of you. The really tough looking inmate with the three little girls, all dressed alike with huge ribbons in their hair, climbing all over him and his tearful wife looking on. There were four or five couples at each visitation where my wife and I were present who were mixed race, either black inmate and white girlfriend or wife or white inmate with a black girlfriend or wife. There were also instances where clearly the inmate's mother was visiting, and she could hardly speak for crying continually during the whole visitation period.

Visitation periods lasted about three hours because the room only held about fifty people and they had to make room for others to visit. Rules for visitation are strict and enforced. The inmate sits on one side of a coffee table and the visitors must sit on the other side. The inmate and visitors can hug and kiss at the beginning of the visit and at the end of the visit, but not touch in between. There are vending machines in the visitation room and the inmate can have whatever they dispense, but he cannot take it back to the barracks. It must be consumed during the visitation period. Since the inmate is not allowed to have coins or any cash, money for the vending machines must be provided by the visitors.

The inmate is pat down searched upon arrival to the visitation area in the entry/exit room where there is also a toilet and sink. Upon leaving, the inmate is strip searched – totally naked – in the same room; usually two or three inmates at the same time. The guard, when you are strip searched, is always male.

Visitation weekends is always something to look forward to, but with some apprehension. We could make all kinds of plans to visit and my wife could arrange for a friend to drive and then on the morning of the visit when she would call the prison, she would be told something like,

"Too foggy, visitation is cancelled for today."

Several times visitation was cancelled because our barracks was being punished, or all of Beaumont Low was being punished. The punishment was incurred due to fights, or some other serious infraction like finding lots of weapons or cell phones during a shakedown. If visitation was cancelled due to punishment, it was always for at least two consecutive weekends so that "even" and "odd" inmates were punished equally.

My last visitation occurred in mid-February 2020. Immediately after the visit, Beaumont Low began to be isolated from the outside world due to the COVID-19 Pandemic. My wife and I would not see each other again until she came to pick me up on March 30, 2020 to take me to Leidel, the halfway house, in Houston. Leidel is 30 miles from my house in southeast Houston as opposed to the 94 miles from my house to Beaumont Low.[46]

---

[46] Leidel — Federal prison halfway house in Houston located at 1819 Commerce Street — Houston, TX 77002.

Chapter XVI
Leidel and Final Thoughts

Leidel – 1819 Commerce St. – Houston, TX

Eventually, like all of life, the passage of time brings a change to one's circumstance. I had gotten use to life in Beaumont Low. There is a routine to prison life and for most inmates, it is a low stress environment. There are few decisions to make and the necessities of life are provided. The barracks was almost always cool to cold, even on the hottest, most humid days. In what passes for winter in southeast Texas, it was comfortable during the coldest months of the year. I learned by experiencing life in prison that there are just ten principles, if followed, lead to a low stress life while in prison; they are:

1. Treat everyone you meet with respect.
2. Develop a Circle of Trust (inmates you find trustworthy and who have a good reputation within the group you are associated with).
3. Avoid inmates who are untrustworthy and/or mentally ill (severely deranged).

4. Minimize contact with inmates in the SO (Sex Offender) section of any barracks.
5. Offer a skill valued by the group. If you do not possess such a skill, develop one.
6. Be loyal to the group.
7. Keep your cell and yourself clean and neat.
8. Help others when you can if it does not compromise your quality of life.
9. Keep your mouth shut most of the time to avoid arguments.
10. Do not loan money (commissary $'s or postage stamps) to anyone not within your Circle of Trust. And even then, only loan money within the circle of trust to those who have a history of paying back loans on time.

There are inmates who never get that your life in prison can be low stress because they do not follow the ten principles of prison life, described above. No one taught these principles to me; I observed and learned them within the first two weeks I was at Beaumont Low. They are the same principles that lead to a low stress life in any institutionalized environment, e.g., army, military school, college, etc.

On March 30, 2020 in the middle of the COVID-19 Pandemic, two of our closest friends drove my wife to Beaumont Low to pick me up and transport me to Leidel. One of many surprises while in custody of the BOP (Federal Bureau of Prisons) is the trust the BOP places on inmates going from prison to a halfway house. The BOP will pay bus fare from the prison to the bus station within walking distance of the halfway house, or they will pay cab fare from the bus station to the halfway house. The commissary money you have when you leave prison is given to you in the form of a debit card. My commissary debit card had a balance of $333.13. Alternatively, a family member or friends can pick you up at the prison and transport you to the halfway house. They gave us four hours to drive about 120 miles from Beaumont Low to Leidel, and I was told to call them if there was an unavoidable delay like a wreck or road maintenance.

Leidel is much nicer than Beaumont Low. Cubicles contain five bunks and they are bigger than the ten-man cell (chicken coop) is at Beaumont Low in UB Barracks. Inmates at the halfway house were for the most part clean and neat. The guards appeared to be the same as at Beaumont Low. Most were nice, a few were mean, and one has earned the nickname, "Nurse Rachet."[47] Nurse Rachet was the only guard that absolutely, strictly followed the rules, and showed no mercy whatsoever to anyone. I heard her in the next cell take an inmate's cell phone because he was listening to radio without earphones. I could not hear it and I was in the neighboring cell. She kept it a week and gave it back to him by throwing it at him while she walked by his cell. She always had a sickening sweet smile on her face when she did something unpleasant to an inmate. In fact, come to think of it, I never saw her do anything pleasant to an inmate. The inmate who had his radio taken for a week by Nurse Rachet said to me one day at lunch,

"Nurse Rachet doesn't seem so bad when she is doing something bad to you if you just visualize her in nothing but black patten leather thigh high stiletto heels and a matching corset."

I thought about it and he was right.

The best part of Leidel is you that can have an iPhone and I could call my wife, or she could call me,

---

[47] Nurse Rachet — a sadistic nurse in the 1975 movie "One Flew Over the Cuckoo's Nest" starring Louise Fletcher as Nurse Rachet (she won the Oscar for Best Actress for the role).

from 6:00 AM until lights out at 10:00 PM seven days a week. The food in comparison to Beaumont Low's chow hall food is excellent. In addition, unless we were being punished, every night from about 5:00 PM until 8:30 PM, we could order food from any commercial establishment that delivered food, including GrubHub and Pizza Hut. On occasion, usually on a weekend, the guards would fire up five BBQ grills in the parking lot and cook hot dogs and hamburgers, just like you would have in your own backyard at home complete with the same condiments you would have at home. The building was always cool to cold even in the hottest weather.

Morning Pill and Sick Call is at 5:00 AM and breakfast is served beginning at 5:15 AM. Mid-day Pill and Sick Call is at Noon and lunch is served, beginning at 12:15 PM. Dinner Pill and Sick Call is at 5:00 PM with dinner beginning to be served at 5:15 PM. There is a final Pill and Sick Call at 9:00 PM. This schedule was adhered to seven days a week unless there were not enough guards to do pill, sick and chow calls all at the same time. If this occurs, it just takes longer because the guard giving out pills or calling the ambulance or handing out food cannot do it all at the same time.

There is a room with vending machines that contains every food item one would want from junk food to really good sandwiches, and you are allowed money to spend on the vending machines. By the vending machines are five commercial microwave ovens to heat water for coffee or the food that you get from the vending machines. The food served for breakfast, lunch and dinner is far above the quality of the food served in the Beaumont Low chow hall. It reminded me of a Wyatt's Cafeteria or the buffet in any restaurant chain that normally has a buffet. There are six washing machines and six driers for each barracks and inmates can use them anytime between 4:00 AM and 10:00 PM seven days a week.

There is a garden area with benches and between the hours of 6:00 AM and 8:30 PM, you could go outside and sit on the benches. Leidel is in downtown Houston so the sounds of nature were often drowned out by traffic noise, but in the early morning birds are singing and there are lots of pigeons, blue jays, doves, cardinals and robins to watch in the trees and grass that surround the benches. This is a refreshing change from the absence of birds, except sea gulls, at Beaumont Low.

Finally, there is a women's barracks at Leidel. Normally, I was told, all barracks ate together, and you could sit together in the garden, but because of the COVID-19 Pandemic precautions, each barracks was isolated from one another and we ate by barracks only and had limited time by barracks in the garden.

Occasionally an individual barracks would be punished, usually for failing to maintain minimum housekeeping standards. And on occasion, all of Leidel would be punished because someone was seen on the security cameras receiving a package over the fence in the garden. The package usually contained liquor or cigarettes. If they could not determine the identity of the inmate who received the package from the video camera, they would punish everyone. Inmates who received packages thrown over the fence would be dressed in gray or blue sweat suits, which is attire common to almost everyone, and it would have a hoody with the hood up. When the package was ready to be thrown over the fence, the inmate would run out to the corner of the fence where it would be thrown and someone else who was in phone contact with the person delivering the package would give the signal to throw it. If timed correctly, the inmate would run out, catch the package when it was thrown and run back in without breaking stride. Yes, it is a game.

If all of Leidel were being punished, the garden would be off limits for three days and the TV's would be disconnected in both the men's and women's TV rooms. The women in Leidel always complained (rightly so) about group punishment; they said,

"You may not be able to tell who it was, but you can always tell it was not a woman!"

They are, of course, correct, but their complaints never resulted in them incurring less punishment than the men.

Getting along with other inmates at Leidel follows the same principles as at Beaumont Low (or any other prison) but was easier because I did not find anyone substantially deranged or criminally insane like at Beaumont Low. Inmates are on their good behavior because if they screw up, it is either a longer time at Leidel or worse, they get shipped back to the prison they came from to serve the remainder of their time in prison instead of a halfway house.

The other difference at Leidel relative to Beaumont Low is that inmates come and go at a faster rate than at the prison. Some inmates only stayed a few nights at Leidel and went on to home confinement. My stay, I believe, is about average, from March 30th to July 16th, 2020; a total of 108 days. My cubicle mates changed partially about every two weeks. One afternoon, Nurse Rachet came in with two other guards and said to my two cubicle mates,

"We're moving you two to other cubicles in dorm B."

There were only three of us in the five-man cubicle in dorm D, cubicle 27 and she was moving my two cubicle mates to dorm B. It seemed she was doing it for no reason other than she could. They had both been there only about one week each and were scheduled to leave within the month. They had just gotten settled. We all wondered, why is she throwing her weight around like this? After grumbling, the guards came in with carts and helped them move their stuff, including their lockers with their possessions kept in them during the move which was unusual. The guards came back with empty lockers to replace the lockers they had moved with the two inmates that were moved out of the cubicle. I wondered why I was blessed with a five-man cubicle all by myself. There was that special feeling again.

The answer came in an ever-growing awareness in me over the next six hours. My new cubicle mates arrived one at a time, all three of them, and they all had four things in common — all were African American, all were over six feet tall and in excellent shape, and all were gay and very effeminate ("flaming" in prison or street jargon). One of the three was a transvestite in the image or RuPaul, except not quite seven feet tall in heels.[48] Each one introduced himself to the others and to me. They talked among themselves at one end of the cubicle and I laid in my bunk reading a murder mystery novel in the middle of the cubicle because I occupied the middle bottom bunk. The transvestite, who called herself, "Fate" who was the tallest of the three was assigned to the bunk above me. There was a single empty bunk at the end of the cubicle. I could tell that some of their conversation was about me and I figured when (or if) they wanted to talk to me they would.

I went to sleep as usual, about 9:30 PM with them still talking. The next morning, I awoke as usual at 4:00 AM when my iPhone alarm went off. I got my shower stuff together and walked out and

---

[48] RuPaul Andre Charles — American drag queen, actor, model, singer, songwriter and television personality.

took a shower. My cubicle mates were all asleep when I left. When I returned, one of them, David, was awake and getting ready to work out in the weight room. David smiled at me and said,

"How much of a problem do you have with us being in here with you?"

Boy, was that ever a loaded question! I had the answer ready though; I said,

"My son is gay, and we have the same excellent relationship we had before he came out. I figured out he was gay about three years before he knew or admitted it to his mother and me. I am out of here and going to home confinement in less than six weeks regardless of who my cubicle mates are. I have no problem with you if you do not have a problem with me."

David smiled and said,

"Sir, the head lady guard [meaning Nurse Rachet] said she was moving us into a cubicle with the most well-respected inmate in here at the moment and there would be no trouble from anyone if we were in here with you."

My opinion of Nurse Rachet went up orders of magnitude. The fact is that these three gay men almost always hung out together and were in better shape and bigger than almost everyone else in the barracks. In addition, I found that even the most homophobic inmate has a survival instinct that outweighs any desire he might have to cause trouble for a gay inmate.

My weirdest moment in all of my stay in the custody of the BOP was at Leidel, not Beaumont Low. After a couple of days, I had become accustomed to my cubicle mates' giggles and primping (hours of looking into a handheld mirror until hair and makeup were perfect). I was amazed that no other inmate ever said anything to me about my cubicle mates; not one word. Anyway, about 10:30 PM on the third or fourth night (I forget which) I was about asleep, and I slowly became aware of two things:

i) From the heavy breathing, cooing and giggling from Fate, my upper bunk mate, I realized she was having phone sex with someone, and
ii) My bunk was rocking back and forth.

All I could think of was, "You can't make this stuff up," and I am sleepy; I hope she gets finished pretty soon. I never mentioned it to her or anyone else while I was at Leidel.

However, the next morning I saw Nurse Rachet was on duty and I waited until she was walking down the hallway by herself. I walked up behind her and said,

"Excuse me, may I please move from the bottom middle bunk to the end single unoccupied bunk?"

Nurse Rachet turned, smiled that sickening sweet smile she always smiled when she was going to do something bad to someone and said,

"Charles, of course you can."

I thanked her, but I refrained from throwing my arms around her and hugging and kissing her for I felt she might take it the wrong way. However, I still pictured her in nothing but black patten leather thigh high stiletto boots and a matching black corset (I still do).

The days counted down until it was time to go — to leave Leidel in the midst of the COVID-19 Pandemic and go to home confinement. While I was at Leidel, four inmates that I know of contracted COVID-19 and went to the hospital, one returned to Leidel, one was released to home confinement and two died. The two that died were in ill health to begin with — diabetes and overweight, plus a lifetime of drug use and a sedentary lifestyle finally caught up with them. COVID-19 was just the final act. One of them that died was in the cubicle across from mine in dorm D where I lived. I said goodbye to him as he was waiting for the ambulance.

The week I was to leave I got tested for COVID-19 and two days later the results came back negative. If it had been positive, I would have had to go to dorm B where they quarantined everyone who tested positive. They had to stay for two weeks in dorm B and then be retested. That was their pattern of existence until they exhibited symptoms and went to the hospital or tested negative and were sent to home confinement.

July 16th finally came, the mathematics works out to 60 percent served at Beaumont Low, 15 percent served at Leidel, and 10 percent served in home confinement. The total percentage is 85 percent; I got 15 percent knocked off for good behavior. I am trying to make this experience a bump in the road of life and not a defining moment.

The transition to home confinement from Leidel was easy. I was fitted with an ankle monitor on my left ankle (I got to choose which ankle I wanted it on). I had to attach a charger at twelve-hour intervals to the ankle monitor which makes it even more cumbersome to wear for the hour or so it takes to charge. Initially, I had to call in three times a day to Leidel from a landline telephone we had to have installed just for this purpose. After thirty days, I was told I only had to call in twice a day. I sat my iPhone alarm to alarm at 8:00 AM, 11:30 AM and 5:30 PM when it was three times a day and deleted the 11:30 AM alarm when it dropped to two times a day. That way, I did not forget to call in. I put the charger on my ankle monitor at the 8:00 AM call and at the 5:30 PM call. On two occasions, a guard in a white, unmarked pickup truck drove up in front of my house while I was in home confinement. He called me on my landline phone and asked me to come out front so he could see me. As soon as I stepped outside, he would wave and drive away. There is that special feeling again.

I thought that finally I was at home and had nothing to do but work on this book until September 25th when I would go back to Leidel and have my ankle monitor removed, then go to my probation officer's office for my initial interview. Then home again and 12-months of probation. It was going to be over!

But No! Hurricane Laura came calling to southeast Texas. I got the call from Leidel on August 25th at 7:00 AM. The guy from Leidel said without any introduction or "good morning"...

"Mr. Callihan, report to Leidel by 9:00 AM due to the possible need to evacuate the area where you live because of Hurricane Laura. Pack clothing and toiletries for four days."

My wife went ballistic; there was crying and tears while I packed. I called one of my closest friends, Andy (not his real name) and said,

"Leidel just called and said I had to return by 9:00 AM with clothing and toiletries for four days. Can you please drive me down there?"

Andy said he could, and that he would be in front of our house at 8:00 AM. While I packed, my wife called the wife of a couple, Mark and Patty (not their real names), we are close friends with and asked if she could stay with them. Of course, they said that she could and sometime after I returned to Leidel, they came and got her and our two dogs. She stayed with them while hurricane Laura visited Beaumont, Lake Charles and communities due north of them. Houston and Seabrook were untouched, and I got to stay another four days (Tuesday through Friday morning) at Leidel.

A lot of the inmates that were at Leidel when I left were either still there or were, like me, forced to return to Leidel from home confinement because they were in the possible path of hurricane Laura. I settled into dorm D cubicle 28 which is next to the one I was in from March 30th until July 16th when I started home confinement. Dorm D cubicle 28 is also closest to the exit door to the garden and I had a window that looked out at the Garden. I judged it to be the best cubicle at Leidel. Leidel had not changed in the five weeks I had been gone. My gay cubicle mates were gone, the really good Barbequed Beef and Philly Cheesesteak sandwiches in the vending machines were also gone. I missed the sandwiches more than I missed "The Ladies," my former cubicle mates, but Daniel returned. Daniel had been a cubicle mate of mine, but he had left just prior to The Ladies arrival. Daniel got his old bunk in cubicle 27 which was the empty single bunk at the end of the cubicle that I had gotten permission from Nurse Rachet to move to just prior to leaving for home confinement.

The four gay men had named themselves "The Ladies" upon their arrival to Leidel. Whenever a female guard enters a dorm, she calls out,

"Female!"

My gay cubicle mates would always in unison respond,

"Hey girl!"

You could hear the groans from some of the other inmates that I suspect were homophobes, but no one tried to harm The Ladies, and no one ever said a word to me about my gay cubicle mates.

Having to go back to Leidel because of the approaching hurricane was, in and of itself, traumatic, but it was heightened by GEO's (the private contractor that manages Leidel and other federal halfway houses in Texas) sad history of how inmates were treated during hurricane Harvey. There is an ongoing lawsuit alleging guards at a GEO managed halfway house, not Leidel, abandoned inmates during hurricane Harvey while the building was flooded with four inches of standing water.[49]

"More than 200 former inmates are suing a private prison contractor who they say 'utterly failed' them during Hurricane Harvey, allegedly leaving the men in a flooded halfway house in Houston surrounded by toxic waste and without food, clean water or medical care. Despite the 'barbaric' conditions, according to the lawsuit, the men couldn't leave the premises because officials told them it would be a violation of their parole."

The afternoon before hurricane Laura was due to arrive Leidel officials were busy setting up generators for each barracks, complete with heavy duty extension cords snaked through windows to

---

[49] https://www.houstonchronicle.com/news/houston-texas/houston/article/Lawsuit-Private-prison-contractor-abandoned-14365055.php

allow lights and a few appliances, like CPAP units, to operate in a power outage. My cubicle was closest to the exit to the garden and the window in my cubicle got one of the extension cords across from my bunk. While I was sitting in the garden, waiting for hurricane Laura to arrive, I remembered that homeless people lived in tents underneath the overpass that you could see from a knothole in the fence on the backside of the garden. I looked through the fence and saw...

Homeless Persons' Tents[50]
(awaiting the arrival of hurricane Laura)

Thursday, August 27th, about 2:00 AM, hurricane Laura made landfall at the Louisiana-Texas state line heading due north at 16 mph. It

---

[50] Not the actual picture, but a close approximation of what I could see through the hole in the fence at Leidel. I got this picture off the internet of homeless peoples' tents under an overpass.

was a Category 4 hurricane when it made landfall, but rapidly weakened to a Category 2, but not before devastating Lake Charles, Port Arthur and neighboring communities still in the recovery mode from hurricane Harvey. Houston and Seabrook suffered no damage at all. So, Friday, August 28th, at 10:00 AM, I got released from Leidel back into home confinement. Mark brought Janice to Leidel and was waiting while I checked out.

They never removed my leg monitor, but they turned it off upon my arrival to Leidel. When it was time for me to return to home confinement, I had to attach a "gadget" to it that took about a minute to program it for my home address. I signed some papers that said I understood that I was still on home confinement and that I could not leave my property and had to call in twice a day just like I was doing four days earlier when I was summoned back to Leidel. I also said a second wave of "goodbyes" to my friends at Leidel, including Nurse Rachet, and a couple of other guards.

Final thoughts...

In the Prologue to this book, I write, "There is no hidden agenda. It is simply my best effort at describing what happened to me..." However, perhaps if there is some learning that can be passed on from this experience, I think it is this...

- ✓ Know that all feelings, good and bad, are temporary. Therefore, suicide is a permanent solution to a temporary feeling.
- ✓ If you want to fit in, no matter where, start by being nice.
- ✓ Keep your mouth shut when confronted with argumentative people.
- ✓ Avoid people, as much as possible, that are mentally unstable.

- ✓ Some people are not capable of changing their Life Cycle.[51] If you are not one of them, just give them advice and do not become too emotionally involved. If you get too emotionally involved with them, it will end badly for you.

A significant portion of inmates I met at Beaumont Low and at Leidel are conspiracy theorists. That is, they see a sinister motive in any bad thing that occurs, from the COVID-19 Pandemic to those people who are not fans of President Trump. Some of them can articulate their theories very eloquently. One of them said,

"The United States incarcerates more people per capita than any other country in the world, including Russia, Iran and North Korea."

I just listened and did not say anything, but I did not believe him. However, I did try to prove him wrong by looking it up on my iPhone, "Incarceration Per Capita by Country" and I got these results. He was right![52]

The top 10 countries incarceration rates per 100,000 population...

---

[51] Life Cycle — The pattern of behaviors and attitude that causes someone to repeat the same mistakes in a never-ending cycle. For example, committing the same crime(s) over and over and serving ever longer prison sentences because of it.

[52] https://worldpopulationreview.com/country-ranking/incarceration-rates-by-country

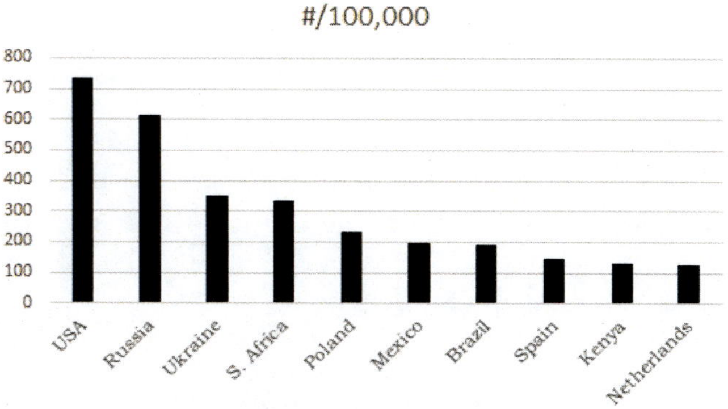

Country	#/100,000	%
USA	737	24
Russia	615	20
Ukraine	350	11
S. Africa	334	11
Poland	235	8
Mexico	196	6
Brazil	193	6
Spain	144	5
Kenya	130	4
Netherlands	128	4

Why are there more per capita inmates in United States federal prisons than say Iran, North Korea or even Russia?[53] Here is why...

[53]https://www.bop.gov/about/statistics/statistics_inmate_offenses.jsp

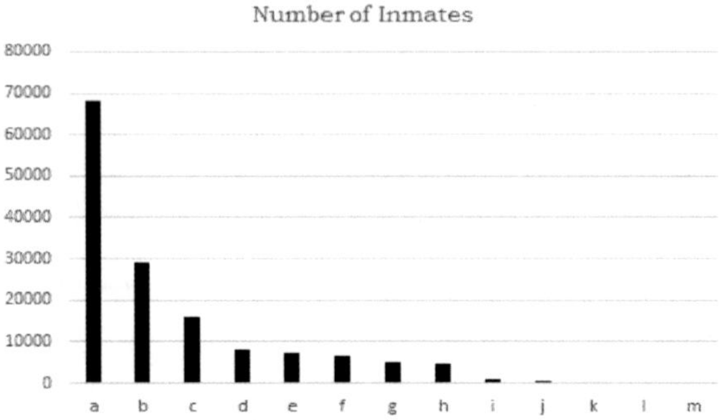

Charge	#	%	Description
a	68167	46.2	Drug Related
b	29252	19.8	Weapons and Arson
c	16030	10.9	Sex Offenses
d	8185	5.5	Extortion, Fraud, Bribery
e	7485	5.1	Burglery, Property Offenses
f	6439	4.4	Immigration
g	5078	3.4	Robbery
h	4812	3.3	Homicide, Assault, Kidnapping
i	934	0.6	Miscellaaneous
j	553	0.4	Courts or Corrections
k	301	0.2	Continuing Criminal Enterprise
l	270	0.2	Counterfeit, Embezzlement
m	43	0.0	National Security

The United States attacks illicit drug usage in the same manner that all countries did, beginning in the 1960's, when the drug problem first became prevalent in the middle class. Note that almost half (46.2%) of the federal prison population is in prison due to drug-related charges. Other countries have improved upon this strategy, but not the United States. For example, one of the biggest differences in German and The Netherlands prisons, relative to the United States, is the focus on "normalization." That is, making life in prison as similar as possible to life on the outside. Germany and The Netherlands prison systems are organized around the central tenets of resocialization and rehabilitation. The United States prison system is organized around the central tenets of incapacitation and retribution. Incarceration is used less frequently and for shorter periods of time in Germany and The Netherlands. Germany and The Netherlands rely heavily on fines or other community-based sentences, and not on not prison sentences.[54]

I am not a crusader. I am an objective observer, and I have objectively observed no one at Beaumont Low or Leidel being "turned around" in their attitudes toward life, society or their own addictions, because of how they were treated while in custody of the Federal Bureau of Prisons, the BOP.

---

[54] https://www.vera.org/publications/sentencing-and-prison-practices

Chapter XVII
What's for dinner and may I see the wine list?

[prison recipes for pizza, apple wine, burritos, chili, seafood pasta, prison bagels and cheesecake]

Another epiphany about prison life was the ingenuity of inmates with little or no formal education and how resourceful they are in lots of different areas. Perhaps the most surprising area, to me anyway, was their ability, without the luxury of decent produce, meat or dairy products, and no access to heat, except for water just below its boiling point, to produce delicious meals. The other surprising aspect of barracks meal preparation was the appearance of some of the best prison chefs.

Prison brings out the extremes of human behavior and appearance. The substantial commonality among the inmate population was the prevalence of tattoos – gang related and plain tattoos. The minority was white guys without tattoos, which included me. Prison chefs were no exception. They were all tattooed and either grossly obese or just the opposite – body builders with Greek God physiques. The other surprising part of prison culture is the high value that skills of all kinds are held. If you could "cook" in the barracks any kind of decent meal with the resources and ingredients available, it did not matter how you looked, what gang you were in or even if you were not a "pure" heterosexual male. Of course, this high regard did not extend to SO's, former guards, policemen or prosecuting attorneys.

Recipes of meals I ate multiple times in the barracks prepared with a stinger and/or the hot water tap, and food smuggled from the chow hall, or purchased from the commissary are presented below; I hope you enjoy them.

Pizza –

1 — 16 oz. (large) bag of corn chips

Punch a small hole in the bag with a ball point pen to let the air out. Take a soap dish and crush the chips in the bag by placing the bag on the floor and putting all of your weight on the soap dish. Move the dish after each "crushing" until there are no more chips to crush. The crushed chips should resemble processed sugar or salt in size and consistency. Add hot water to the bag through the hole and mix until the consistency of pizza dough is obtained. Take the "dough" out of the bag and spread on a locker top/grill that has been cleaned.

1 — package of pepperoni

Open the package and spread the pepperoni evenly on the dough that has been spread into the round or square shape of a pizza and is about one fourth inch thick.

Shredded cheese

Add cheese of whatever kind was smuggled from the chow hall. Parmesan powder from the commissary can also be used. Add as much cheese as either you have, or you want.

Tomatoes or tomato paste

Add tomatoes ground into a paste, or if tomato paste smuggled from the chow hall is available, use it.

Polish Sausage

Polish sausage is good on pizza and is available from the commissary. Slice the Polish sausage with a shiv (described in footnote 15 in the Apple Wine section) or leave it in its package and stomp on it with your boots on so it is smashed and can be spread on the pizza like tomato paste.

Louisiana Hot Sauce

All barracks meals are made better via the addition of a generous amount of Louisiana Hot Sauce. It is as common as ketchup at McDonalds for meals prepared in the barracks. For some inmates, there is no such thing as too much Louisiana Hot Sauce on any food, regardless of where it was prepared, or what it is.

Place a clear plastic trash bag over the pizza and put another locker top/grill on top of the trash bag. Add hot water from the hot water tap or from a bucket that has been heated to boiling by a stinger to the top locker/grill. After fifteen minutes, replace the water with fresh hot water for another fifteen minutes. After thirty minutes of this hot water "cooking" the cheese will be melted, and the pizza will be hot and ready to eat. Seasoned beef, normally used for tacos, which comes in a packet from the commissary can also be added or substituted for the pepperoni, if preferred.

Apple Wine –

Collect about three dozen apples from the chow hall. Collect cinnamon from the prison bakery and from oatmeal condiments. Smuggle yeast from the prison bakery. Baker's yeast comes in one quarter pound squares; it looks like a gray stick of butter and smells, you guessed it, like yeast. Slice the apples as finely as possible with a shiv you have made from a toothbrush and disposable razor blade.[55] Take a clean, clear plastic trash bag and spread it on the floor. Spread the cut or diced apples into the middle of the trash bag so when the apples are further crushed the juice stays on the trash bag. Take a clean locker top/grill and place over the apples and have the heaviest guy in the cell stand on the locker top/grill and rock back and forth so the apples are crushed. Collect the crushed apples and juice by lifting all four sides of the trash bag at once. Pour it into a wastebasket lined with another clear trash bag. Add the yeast – four one quarter inch thick squares to the wastebasket. Add the cinnamon to the wastebasket, if you like the taste of cinnamon in the apple wine. Cover the wastebasket with the ends of the trash bag lining the

---

[55] shiv – take one toothbrush, a roll of electrical tape from the prison electrical shop or prison vocational technical school where they teach you to be an electrician, and one disposable razor. Stomp on the razor with your boots on so it is crushed, and the razor blade is free from its plastic housing. Tape one third of the razor blade to the end of the handle of the toothbrush. You have just made a shiv. A shiv is useful for defending yourself, attacking another inmate, for food preparation, or for hiding it under someone else's mattress and then anonymously leaving a note for the guard that so-and-so has a shiv under his mattress. That will get so-and-so six months in the SHU and loss of his good time days.

wastebasket. You can also place the wastebasket in another trash bag for further protection.

Guards will confiscate this, so it must be well hidden. The best place to hide it in UB barracks, and probably the equivalent space in any of the barracks at Beaumont Low, is the space above the drop ceiling in the communal shower area. There is a four feet tall space above the drop ceiling and below the cement of the floor above. This space houses pipes and electrical wiring. It is also full of black mold and cockroaches. Guards do not like darkness, mold and cockroaches so it is an ideal space to hide things that guards will confiscate.

Every three days open the bag to vent it and stir the contents. After about three weeks, or whenever there is no need to vent the bag, it is ready to filter. Filtering is necessary to remove the pieces of apple that are still in the bag as well as any cockroaches that inadvertently find their way into the bag. A filter is made from a well-used pillowcase. It must be well-used because if it is new, the dye in the pillowcase (bedding is all dark brown) will bleed into the apple wine and ruin its color and taste.

Three dozen large apples yield about one gallon of apple wine. The wine is placed into a cleaned bleach jug labeled, "Clorox" and placed alongside cleaning fluids in the mop closet. Guards tend to believe labels on containers in the mop closet, so it is as safe as it can be. Besides, it was usually gone by the end of the first night of availability. Vintage of wine in a prison barracks refers to the day it is opened, and not to the year the fruit from which it was made was harvested.

Burritos —

1 — package of dehydrated ramen beef or chicken noodle soup
1 — 8 oz. bag of Jalapeno flavored corn chips
¼ — cup of Cheese Whiz (spray cheese)
Louisiana Hot Sauce (of course)
1 — 8 oz. bag of Cheetos
1 — flour tortilla
1 — packet of seasoned taco beef or chicken
1 — 2 flour tortillas

Crush the ramen noodles in the bag before opening. You can throw them on the concrete floor of your cell several times. There is a fine line between throwing them hard enough to break them into small pieces and not so hard that the bags break and spreads them all over the floor. I never quite got the hang of it, so I was not allowed to throw the noodles on the floor after I broke two bags during two different burrito preparation times. Place the ramen noodles, still in the bag in hot water either from the hot water tap or the mop bucket that has been "stingered." While the noodles are cooking, crush the corn chips, and Cheetos using a clean trash bag on the floor and the soap dish described in the recipe for making pizza dough by crushing corn chips. Add the Cheese Whiz to the crushed corn chips and Cheetos to the consistency of burrito filling. Add the cooked ramen noodles to the mixture along with the seasoned taco beef or chicken. Lay out the tortillas and add the filling to them.

Recommended: For an extra special treat that is also exiting since you might get electrocuted and/or start a fire, heat a gallon of cooking oil or pure butter, if you have smuggled enough butter from the chow hall, in a clean bucket or the lower half of a plastic bleach jug via the Charles Stinger and deep fry the burrito. This is the best way of enjoying your prison burritos.

Chili –
1 — 8 oz. can of Manwich
1 — packet of seasoned taco meat

Open the can of Manwich and the packet of seasoned taco meat. Do not drain the taco meat. Combine both in a Tupperware bowl available from the commissary. Place the Tupperware bowl in a bath of water and heat the water with a stinger, Charles Stinger, or regular stinger. Serve with club crackers, Fritos, or corn chips. It is especially good with Apple Wine.

NOTE: As an alternative meat, cooked hamburger patties, smuggled from the chow, hall can be broken into pieces and substituted for seasoned taco meat, or added as an additional meat, in this recipe.

Seafood Pasta —
4 — large packages (4 servings per package) of dehydrated chicken noodle soup [alternative 6 regular sized (2 serving per package)]
2 — beef sausages
4 — packages of mackerel
1 — medium onion
1 — green pepper

1. Open noodle soup packages, discard seasoning packets.
2. Place noodles in large trash bag.
3. Add hot water (200°F) from the hot water tap until it just covers the noodles and set aside for 10 minutes. An alternative is to use the Charles Stinger and heat two gallons of water to a boil in five minutes in a clean mop bucket.
4. Chop onions, peppers, sausages, and mackerel with a shiv (see how to make a shiv in footnote for apple wine). The pieces should be a little larger than diced pieces.
5. Drain the noodles into another trash bag that has pin holes in it, so the water drains out. Add hot water to the noodles and let it drain again (you are washing away surface starch so the noodles will not cling to one another).
6. Repeat step 5 (at least once).
7. Transfer noodles to six serving bowls in equal amounts.
8. Add the onions, peppers, sausages, and mackerel from step 4 in equal amounts to the six-serving bowls with the noodles in them.
9. Place each bowl in hot water (like a double boiler) for five minutes, covered, but not tight.

NOTE: The hot water/double boiler is made from a mop bucket with the Charles Stinger in it. Cover the top of the double boiler with a trash bag to conserve heat.

10. Add butter, three pats per bowl and stir.
11. Add Louisiana Hot Sauce to taste for each bowl.

Serves six.

Prison Bagels —
4 — bagels
1 — 8 oz. packet of jalapeno pepper cream cheese
1 — package pepperoni
1 — package grated Mexican three cheeses
1 — bottle of Louisiana Hot Sauce

1. Slice bagels with a shiv (see footnote on how to make a shiv in footnote for apple wine).
2. Spread each bagel slice with jalapeno cream cheese.
3. Spread pepperoni slices on top of jalapeno cream cheese.
4. Spread Mexican three cheeses on top of pepperoni.
5. Place sheet of wax paper on top of each bagel slice.
6. Place clothes iron which is turned on high on top of each bagel slice until the cheese is thoroughly melted.

Serves four.

Cheesecake —
6 — pats of butter
1 — 8 oz. package of Graham crackers, vanilla wafers or Oreos
6 oz. of non-dairy coffee creamer
4 cups of vanilla pudding
12 oz. of lemon or lime juice
1 — 8 oz. package of cream cheese

1. Melt the butter by placing it in a coffee cup and place the coffee cup in a Tupperware bowl with hot water. Change the water, if necessary, until the butter is completely liquified.

2. Mix the liquified butter with crushed crackers, wafers and/or Oreos. Crush them as described for making pizza dough.
3. Line a Tupperware bowl with the crushed crackers, wafers and/or Oreos and butter to form a crust for the cheesecake filling.
4. Place the Tupperware with the crust in an ice bath formed by taking ice from the ice machine (all barracks at Beaumont have ice machines).
5. Combine water with non-dairy coffee creamer and the packet of cream cheese to the consistency of pie filling. Note that in a pinch, you do not have to have cream cheese. You can just use more non-dairy coffee creamer to make the filling, but the cream cheese does make it better. However, cream cheese is not always available, but non-dairy coffee creamer is almost always available.

Made in the USA
Columbia, SC
21 August 2024

5af554b0-e470-45ee-9bc6-7475f6a47624R01